"*The Hospitable Leader* presents a meaningful new approach to leadership that is sure to improve the organizations that embrace it. Terry Smith's deep commitment to moral leadership, dignity, and diversity shine through on every page."

—Jack and Suzy Welch, bestselling authors and cofounders of the Jack Welch Management Institute

"By far, this is one of the most inspiring leadership books I have read in a decade. Terry writes beautifully of the unspoken longings hidden away in most leaders' hearts . . . to lead so others will thrive as they travel with us and to inspire others to a level of trust and faith that ultimately draws God near to the kingdoms of their hearts. Terry's *The Hospitable Leader* is a unique blend . . . part Dallas Willard, part Winston Churchill, part Mother Teresa, but completely unique. Terry Smith is a wordsmith with a gift for igniting a passion that makes us long to become the leaders God created us to be. You. Will. Love. This. Book!"

—Valerie Bell, CEO, Awana Clubs International

"Terry Smith is an extraordinary leader and communicator. *The Hospitable Leader* is Terry at his best as a thinker, writer, and leader. He and his church embody the art of hospitality as well as any church I've ever met in thirty years. This is a fantastic and important read."

—Dr. Mac Pier, founder and CEO, The NYC Leadership Center

"Joel Osteen and I count it an honor to have access to Terry Smith's leadership insight and impartation. Terry is a pastor, life teacher, business consultant, philosopher, futurist, and confidant to a wide circle of influential leaders in this country. No hype: This may be the most important book on leadership I have read in more than a decade."

—Phil Munsey, chairman, Champions Network and Joel Osteen Ministries

"Hospitality and leadership are not often words that coincide, but this book proves how the ideas are inseparable. *The Hospitable Leader* gives a welcome look into how these principles should play out in our lives."

—Mark Batterson, lead pastor, National Community Church, Washington, DC, and bestselling author of *The Circle Maker*

"Pastor Terry has certainly had a positive influence on my life as a father, husband, and leader through his ministry at TLCC. He lives each day as an example of a hospitable leader, and I know he will have the same impact for readers of this book."

—Roman Oben, vice president, Youth Football, National Football League, and Super Bowl XXXVII Champion

"Here's a gentle reminder that leading effectively can be enhanced by including the heart as well as the head. Be prepared to see how caring, warm relationships can surpass technology and tactics as approaches to extraordinary organizational success. Breaking bread together may accomplish more than harsh words and demanding quotas."

—Dan Miller, *New York Times* bestselling author of *48 Days to the Work You Love*

"I have known Terry Smith for a long time and if anyone can speak to the topic of leadership and hospitality it is certainly him. A visit to The Life Christian Church has always been a pleasure and I've always brought it back to the hospitality. There is an atmosphere of 'being at home.' Terry and his wife, Sharon, set that atmosphere."

—Willie Alfonso, chaplain, New York Yankees & Staten Island Yankees

"I have had the honor to call Terry Smith my friend for many years. I have seen him live out these principles of leadership in his life. *The Hospitable Leader* easily guides you to the next level you desire to get to."

—Matthew Barnett, *New York Times* bestselling author and cofounder, Los Angeles Dream Center

"Terry Smith knows what it takes to become the kind of leader people want to follow, and in *The Hospitable Leader* he shares the surprising keys to creating environments where people thrive and realize their God-inspired dreams. Whether you're a CEO, pastor, or parent, you will be equipped to adopt this unique leadership paradigm and unleash the power it brings to effectively influence others."

—Tommy Barnett, copastor, Dream City Church,
Phoenix; cofounder, Los Angeles Dream Center;
author of *The Power of a Half Hour*

"Reading this delightful book put a smile on my face and stirred up a desire in me to become a more hospitable leader. I had never strung together the words *hospitable* and *leader* but now I see how beautifully they go together."

—Nancy Beach, leadership coach, Slingshot Group, and author of
Gifted to Lead: The Art of Leading as a Woman in the Church

"*The Hospitable Leader* is a practicum on leadership and teaching built on the twenty-six years Terry Smith spent building and equipping leaders in one of the most diverse churches in the United States. My success as a professor in 'the greatest urban university in the world' is based on these principles."

—Maria Rice Bellamy, Ph.D., associate professor of literature,
City University of New York, and author of *Bridges to Memory:
Postmemory in Contemporary Ethnic American Women's Fiction*

"In my frequent travels, I have rarely met a leader and a church more hospitable. I am thrilled that Terry is sharing some of his secrets to hospitality with other leaders and churches. Hospitality is one of those underrated biblical concepts, and yet it has the potential to transform our workplaces and churches in ways that make the warmth of the Gospel more accessible for the people who need it the most."

—Matt Brown, evangelist, author, and founder, Think Eternity

"Terry Smith wants the church of Jesus Christ to shine for Him! But in his new book *The Hospitable Leader* he wisely points out that the message must always include the kindness, encouragement, and compassionate understanding that everyone needs. His book will both inform and inspire you!"

—Jim Cymbala, senior pastor, The Brooklyn Tabernacle

"Terry Smith has once again written a cutting-edge leadership book that engages both mind and heart. On numerous occasions I have been blessed to personally witness the principles set forth in *The Hospitable Leader* as I visited the church he leads. With this thoughtful and captivating offering, I now have a much greater insight into how the richness of the diverse culture was intentionally created. This is a must-read for leaders desiring to glean new insight on creating a hospitable environment."

—Dan Dean, lead singer, Phillips, Craig, and Dean, and lead pastor, Heartland Church, Carrollton, Texas

"In *The Hospitable Leader*, Terry Smith challenges leaders to create positive environments, and transform the inhospitable places. No matter the place or position, the climate we set as leaders matters. This read will enrich the heart of any organization."

—Chris Durso, author of *The Heist: How Grace Robs Us of Our Shame*

"Wow! *The Hospitable Leader* is more than a book—it is a guide, a total paradigm shift for leaders. It masterfully captures the leadership of Jesus, which makes it captivating. Every sentence evokes a big YES deep down in your soul. It's the simplicity of this concept that makes it so profound. It takes something you knew but had tucked away, like an old recipe brought back to be the star of the meal. Great job!!!"

—Maria Durso, pastor, Christ Tabernacle, Glendale, New York

"Given the constant expectations and demands on leaders, being hospitable can be easily overlooked. Yet, it's a prerequisite for effective leadership. Using clear, simple language, Terry Smith provides us with tools to help us excel in creating a hospitable culture for those we lead. His leadership take-homes at the end of every chapter will make you a 'doer.' *The Hospitable Leader* is an enjoyable must-read for anyone aspiring to influence others for the Kingdom of God."

—Michael Durso, senior pastor, Christ
Tabernacle, Glendale, New York

"In a world torn apart by animosity and polarization, we need more hospitable leaders! Practical and substantive, this book invites us to lead well by first serving well, opening our doors to our neighbors, and embracing a much more welcoming picture of home."

—Peter Greer, president and CEO, HOPE International,
and coauthor of *Rooting for Rivals*

"Terry Smith has found a hidden ingredient in successful leadership: hospitality. We have all known driven, angry, overbearing, or controlling leaders in our lifetimes. It's sad, but a kind, inclusive, hospitable leader is far too rare. Terry lays out a formula found in the ancient wisdom of the Scriptures that seems modern and new. I not only fully recommend reading but also applying *The Hospitable Leader* to your life. You will go further and be happier and more fulfilled doing it!"

—Mike Hayes, president, Churches in Covenant and the Center for
National Renewal Initiative; founding pastor, Covenant Church

"*The Hospitable Leader* echoes Peter Drucker's insight, 'Good manners are the lubricating oil of an organization.' Mr. Smith will open new doors with his values-based words."

—Frances Hesselbein, former CEO of the Girl Scouts of
the USA; recipient of the Presidential Medal of Freedom;
chairman, The Frances Hesselbein Leadership Forum

"In *The Hospitable Leader*, Terry Smith has served up fantastic food for thought and leadership nuggets. Get ready for a fresh approach to leadership and life that is inviting and enticing to others while growing the reader with applicable truths and tools. Terry's entertaining and intellectual approach, blended with years of hands-on hospitable leadership, makes this book a must-have for every leader's bookshelf."

—Scott R. Jones, senior pastor, Grace Church, Humble, Texas

"Terry Smith has discovered the power contained in a welcome. And now *The Hospitable Leader* is available to all of us and provides a practical roadmap for building a hospitable and welcoming organization, church, or business. Making people feel welcome is vital for all of us, regardless of where we live and work. Terry and the team at The Life Christian Church do this incredibly well!"

—Brad Lomenick, former president, Catalyst, and author of *The Catalyst Leader* and *H3 Leadership*

"Leadership is multifaceted. If you've been leading for any length of time, you know this. In *The Hospitable Leader*, Terry shines an important light on the value of hospitality in leadership and the power of what happens when it's a central part of who we are as leaders. If you think hospitality is simply a task for your team, you're missing this."

—Carey Nieuwhof, founding pastor, Connexus Church

"If his notion of hospitable leadership is not universally taught now, it should be. Pastor Terry Smith carefully and clearly outlines a leadership style that is too often absent in this modern world. A blueprint for both people in leadership and for all of us in our daily lives."

—Robert Parisi, mayor, Township of West Orange, New Jersey

"After fifteen-plus years of working in the Church and in business, I've seen the power in paying attention to hospitality and creating a welcoming environment for everyone. The crazy thing about this is that so many people do not do this successfully or see it as a leadership issue. It's 100 percent a leadership decision, and I'm so thankful for my good friend Terry Smith diving into the power of this principle!"

—Tyler Reagin, president, Catalyst

"*The Hospitable Leader* by Pastor Terry—a must-read to be a WINNING leader! It is practical, inspirational, and definitely timely. This is taking leadership to the next dimension. Not just IQ + EQ but demonstrating love, compassion, and grace as a leader, with Jesus as our example!"

—Jenny Sim, vice president, Global Sourcing, Foot Locker

"All readers, whatever their leadership level or spiritual bent, will find much to stimulate their thinking in this book. Its breadth and elegant simplicity, the various leadership tenets explored, and the soundness of concepts will stir both the heart and mind. As Terry has done throughout his career, he helps us again think more clearly about ways to lead."

—Tony Steadman, transformation lead,
Americas Organization, Ernst & Young

"Regardless of whether you are a CEO, a line supervisor in a factory, a teacher, a service provider, a parent, or a student, *The Hospitable Leader* has something for everyone. Pastor Terry does a remarkable job in explaining to us how to lead hospitably, while showing us, by example after example, how Jesus did the same."

—Paul Theodore, president and CEO, Visual Graphic Systems

"Terry has an incredible way of guiding the reader through what it means to be a true leader. This book is a go-to for anyone who is interested in becoming a stronger team member and overall leader in their organization."

—Jarrid Wilson, pastor and author of *Love Is Oxygen*

THE
HOSPITABLE
LEADER

THE HOSPITABLE LEADER

CREATE ENVIRONMENTS WHERE PEOPLE AND DREAMS FLOURISH

TERRY A. SMITH

BETHANYHOUSE
a division of Baker Publishing Group
Minneapolis, Minnesota

To the people of TLCC:
You are the most hospitable leaders I know.

Contents

Contents

Invitation

On the shelf behind me, as I write this, are some of the best books ever written about leadership. On another shelf are some of the best books ever written about hospitality. I imagine—and I do have a fertile imagination—that if these two shelves got married, this book might be their offspring: the best qualities of leadership and hospitality commingled in one descendant. Over the course of this book I'd like to share with you how this combination can change your life and the lives of those around you.

I may seem like an unlikely person to write about hospitable leadership inasmuch as I have been leading for many years in a place not well known for its warmhearted hospitality. Do you remember the Frank Sinatra song celebrating the challenge and possibility of New York City? He sang, "If I can make it there, I'll make it anywhere." I love to hear that song blaring over the loud speakers as I leave Yankee Stadium with my family after a Yankees win. But in the past twenty-six years or so I have also heard it play over and over in my mind as I have faced the complexities inherent in trying to lead something great in a New Jersey suburb of New York City. Sinatra—who grew up in New Jersey not far from where I live and lead—could sell the message of this song not only because of his sublime talent, but because he got it. If you can make it here, you just might be able to make it anywhere.

This book is about how to lead in all kinds of places, but it flows out of my experience leading in a famously inhospitable place. You know what I mean: Our national spokesman for some time was our bombastic former governor, famous for his YouTube tirades and bridge closings. I was honored to meet him—and in person he really is a nice guy. But like most things New Jersey, the public presentation is loud and in-your-face.

Our most famous businessman may be a television character named Tony Soprano. When people hear *Jersey Shore*, they think not of the 141 miles of beautiful boardwalks and beaches that New Jersey natives treasure, but a beyond-crass reality TV show. Somebody said that our state bird is a hand signal and our state song is a honking horn. And though, in fact, our state nickname—the Garden State—is a perfect description of New Jersey's natural beauty, people talk much more about how property taxes are ridiculously high and how far too many of our politicians are infamously corrupt. Late-night comedians drop New Jersey jokes like our trees drop leaves in the fall (though some are lucky enough to live here).

It drives me a little crazy, to be frank. Yes, we are the most densely populated state in the nation, and we have our share of challenges. But we also have one of the highest per capita income levels, and sit in the shadow of the greatest city in the world, with all the wonders it affords. Okay. I'm getting defensive here. My point is that though I passionately love this place and its people, New York City and its New Jersey suburbs are not known for a particularly hospitable climate in almost any way.

Look, I'll take New Jersey people any day. They are so real! When they say they love you, they really love you. When you make a friend, you have a friend for life. Underneath it all, people are genuinely gracious and kind. It just seems that we might never want anyone to know it. But I have to acknowledge that when folks around the country talk about Southern hospitality, they are not referring to the South Bronx or South Jersey.

Here's the deal: I have learned—and am learning—how to be a hospitable leader in what many believe is an inhospitable place. I know, however, that most of us lead in an inhospitable setting at some time and place in our lives. The finest corporation experiences challenging periods during the normal ups and downs of organizational life cycles. The most profitable small business must survive seasons facing economic head winds. The healthiest family suffers times of turbulence. The winningest coach must

> **We can create the conditions for good and great things to happen. Any time. Any place.**

lead teams with less talent than needed to win during some seasons. The finest teachers have to practice their craft in less than favorable learning environments at some point. The most gifted pastor attempts to shepherd a congregation to unity and growth during times when it feels like everything in this world and beyond fights every effort to do good.

Let's face it: The whole world can feel a little inhospitable at times. But that's okay—we can create the conditions for good and great things to happen. Any time. Any place. Through this book, I want to help leaders make positive environments better and transform the most difficult settings into hospitable places.

Jesus modeled hospitable leadership in so many ways. I am particularly inspired by His description of His kingdom as a feast that a king prepared for his son. How many leaders could describe their leadership sphere in such hospitable terms? I suggest that we think of our leadership in this way: as a feast we are throwing for our followers—stockholders, teams, employees, customers, congregants, students, children. Jesus did the most important work for the world, and led the most successful movement in the history of the world, in the context of a radical hospitality—a feast He made ready and to which everyone is invited.

Hospitality was not optional for the earliest leaders of the Christian church. They were required to practice hospitable leadership, and their hospitality is part of the reason they were able to continue to provide leadership for the most successful movement in history.

The apostle Paul wrote to his protégé Timothy that a leader is to be hospitable or "he must enjoy having guests in his home." He told Christians in Rome that they must "practice hospitality." The apostle Peter told the church at large to "offer hospitality to one another without grumbling." And the writer to the Hebrews was clear: "Do not forget to show hospitality."

Hospitable leaders view life and leadership through the lens of hospitality. They aspire to create environments of welcome where moral leadership can be exercised in all of its permutations. These environments can be physical—even a literal feast, perhaps—but even more they are spiritual, attitudinal, and communicative.

We should see hospitable leadership as a worldview, a mindset, an approach. It can have multiple expressions in action and behavior. We should think of it as a philosophical operating system. A great operating system helps everything work better, both independently and in relation to others. If we can view all of our activities through the lens of hospitality, I think our leadership might feel like a feast that we prepare for everyone in our domain.

Let me show you one of the many ways this plays out in my leadership context. I am the lead pastor of The Life Christian Church in northern New Jersey. Perhaps the thing the congregation is best known for is its incredible diversity. We are a beautiful mosaic of all kinds of people. We do not have a dominant racial group. We are black and brown and white and every imaginable variation thereof. We come from a multitude of nations of origin. We are rich and all levels of not so rich. We are PhDs and GEDs. We are young and not so young. We are Catholics, Baptists, Presbyterians, Pentecostals, Lutherans, Methodists—and lots of previously unchurched people. When people visit us—especially from other parts of the country—they are often blown away. Several years ago, an internationally recognized pastor who has addressed churches and leaders all over the world spoke for us. When he saw the diversity of our congregation, he said, "It took my breath away." Frankly, that's pretty typical of what people say about us.

We should see hospitable leadership as a worldview, a mindset, an approach.

When I am asked, "How have you grown such a diverse congregation? And how do you lead it now?" my response is, "Hospitable leadership." This book is an attempt to explain what I mean when I say that.

For now, suffice it to say the hospitality I propose is a way of approaching everything. Yes, there is a physicality to hospitable leadership. We have developed a beautiful broadcast campus on a major throughway thirteen miles from Times Square, with a pond, waterfall, fountains, coffee bar, fireplace, and other requisite hospitable stuff. We have warm, happy, and well-trained first-impressions people, as do many churches and other organizations. But we were hospitable during the long seventeen years we spent in a storefront Worship and Mission Center—contiguous with the Liquor Lobby on one side and Pauley's Pub on the other—just off main street. With not one parking space we could call our own. We did the best we could with that old bowling-alley-turned-printing-factory-turned-church. But if hospitable primarily means physical space, we were severely limited for a long time. So how did we grow such a large, thriving, diverse congregation in such an inhospitable physical setting? We created the conditions—in a multiple of ways—in which every imaginable kind of person could be welcomed and led to a better life. In this book I want to share some of what we have learned.

I think it is important to say that I hear more and more really good leadership practitioners and theorists talk about leadership in a manner that sounds like a feast to me—leaders who talk about leadership in terms of love, who truly serve their followers, and who work hard to create organizational cultures that care for people as a primary part of organizational mission. I humbly submit *The Hospitable Leader* as a means to describe a leadership zeitgeist of sorts—something that is already happening, increasingly, through some stellar leaders and outstanding organizations. I have learned from so many who are leading hospitably without, perhaps, ever having heard the term *hospitable leader.*

I also observe that on the other hand, there is a proliferation of a kind of leadership that can most hospitably be described as inhospitable. The result is an increasing ugliness and polarization in our world. I think people are longing for more hospitable leaders who create a climate of invitation and welcome that allows all kinds of people to work together in unity to heal the brokenness that is all around us. Hopefully this book will serve as an invitation to be part of a movement of hospitable leaders.

The Hospitable Leader is organized into five Welcomes. **Welcome One: Home** more fully introduces the concept of hospitable leadership and makes the case that productive hospitality is rooted in the idea of home and warm hearts. **Welcome Two: Strangers** invites you to consider the revolutionary possibilities of practicing a radical hospitality that welcomes every stranger as a potential messenger from God and offers resistance to the relational division in our world. **Welcome Three: Dreams** alerts us to the opportunity to be intentionally hospitable to dreamers and their dreams and to help their dreams come true in their Area of Destiny. **Welcome Four: Communication** clarifies that hospitality is not a vague sentimentality but that hospitable communicators create space where transformative truth can be spoken. **Welcome Five: Feasts** speaks to the leader's state of being and shows us that if our leadership is going to feel like a feast, then we must learn to be intentional about hope and happiness and enjoy the feast of life.

I welcome you into exploring and applying these ideas that have changed my life and the lives of so many others who offer me the privilege of serving them. I hope you sense something warm and welcoming—something that invites you in—through the words I have written. I desperately want to be a hospitable leader—a hospitable communicator—who through this book creates space that helps you lead more and more successfully in all kinds of times and places.

Sources

"If I can make it there": Frank Sinatra, vocalist, "Theme from *New York, New York*," by John Kander and Fred Ebb, *Trilogy: Past Present Future*, 1980, Reprise.

"he must enjoy having guests": 1 Timothy 3:2 NLT.

"practice hospitality": Romans 12:13.

"offer hospitality to one another without grumbling": 1 Peter 4:9.

"Do not forget to show hospitality.": Hebrews 13:2.

HOME

1

The Hospitable Leader

A hospitable leader creates environments of welcome where moral leadership can more effectively influence an ever-expanding diversity of people.

I confess that I am not often powerfully moved when visiting a museum. My favorite collection is often found in the café. But Renaissance painter Paolo Veronese grabbed my heart with *The Wedding Feast at Cana*.

My wife, Sharon, and I, along with our son Caleb, were in Paris for a few days of holiday and learning. We made the obligatory visit to the Louvre and thoroughly enjoyed exploring the largest art museum in the world. We made certain not to miss seeing the *Mona Lisa*—arguably the most famous painting on this planet. I was incredulous when we walked into the room where it is displayed: Da Vinci's masterpiece was celebrated like a rock star. A scrum of people surged as close as possible to the surprisingly small painting. So many pictures were being taken and videos shot, it was as if we were in a room full of paparazzi.

I probably shouldn't admit it, but I was a little underwhelmed. The *Mona Lisa* is beautiful, but it looked small and distant on the large and otherwise empty wall.

Then I saw it. On the opposite wall was the largest painting in the Louvre: *The Wedding Feast at Cana*. This is the painting the *Mona Lisa* looks at. There on a gargantuan canvas, with warm light emanating from His head, sat Jesus, the focal point of a great banquet. And He was looking right at me. Of the more than one hundred guests at this sumptuous feast, He was the only one looking at me. I felt like He was inviting me in. Welcoming me.

Veronese seemed to feel this welcome when he created his astounding work of art. Part of what fascinates me is who he placed with Jesus at this wedding celebration. Mary and some of the apostles surround Jesus at the center of the table. But Veronese also included known historical figures, as well as some of his contemporaries, family, and close personal friends. And . . . he included himself. All of them are speechless and sated as they drink wine of eternal vintage in the presence of the Miracle Maker himself.

I was so moved as I stood before that stunning scene. I wanted to shout at the museum crowd, "You are focused on the wrong thing! Or at least the lesser thing! As beautiful as the *Mona Lisa* is, you should turn and look at what she looks at all day." There, on the largest canvas in the largest museum in the world, was the greatest leader in the history of the world inviting us to a feast. And no one was paying attention.

To be fair, as I looked at the scene before me, I had some sense of what it represented. I had thought about it for years. I knew that Jesus had introduced himself to the world at this wedding celebration. That when He turned water into wine to gift a newly married couple and to satisfy and amaze all of their guests, it was the first indication of who He was and what He came to do. As John wrote in his gospel account of this feast,

"What Jesus did here in Cana of Galilee was the first of the signs through which he revealed his glory."

Furthermore, on that day in Paris, I had been in a season of thought and research concerning a new way of thinking about leadership. I was so discouraged with so much of the leadership I was seeing in the world around me. I knew I was not alone in this. I believed—and I believe this now even more than I did then—that our world aches for a new kind of leadership. For a new kind of leader. And there in the Louvre, that leader sat looking right at me. Revealing to the world that a new kind of leader had, in fact, arrived. A leader who would change everything and do it while inviting all of us in. Who would welcome us—in ways great and small—to follow Him. To join Him in His mission. At that moment I realized that Jesus was the prototype of the new kind of leader our world needs. A hospitable leader. Jesus is the ultimate hospitable leader.

The most successful leader in the history of the world led in a context of hospitality. Jesus often used—or created—hospitable environments to welcome people to himself and employ them in His mission. Again, one of the ways He described His kingdom was as a wedding feast that a king prepared for his son. A feast to which everyone is invited. How many kings would ever have described their kingdoms in this way? How many of us who lead could describe our leadership in terms of a feast?

We can learn about hospitable leadership by extrapolating from the leadership story of Jesus. We can also learn from many leaders who have led hospitably in many settings through history, down to our time. We can each learn to cultivate climates that feel like a feast, where those we are leading are welcomed in, and where we can practice other tried and proven leadership theories more effectively than ever before.

Hospitable leadership does not replace other successful leadership methods—it supplements them. Hospitable leaders intentionally create environments where all of our leadership efforts are enhanced. We should hope for our leadership to look more and more like the leadership of Jesus—the most remarkable leader who ever lived.

It is astounding to see just how much the leadership story of Jesus happened in relation to hospitality. Though I suppose we shouldn't be surprised. As Tim Chester explains, there are only three ways the Gospels complete the sentence "the Son of Man came. . . ." Two explain *why* He came. They speak to His mission: "to seek and to save the lost" and "to serve others and to give his life as a ransom for many." The third describes *how* He came. It speaks to the means He used to fulfill His mission. Jesus said it himself: "The Son of Man came eating and drinking." He fulfilled His mission in a framework of feasting, welcome, and invitation—hospitality.

When we create hospitable environments, it increases the likelihood that people will receive our leadership efforts. Leaders—especially in today's world—must seek permission from followers in order to lead them. We must invite people in. We must welcome them to the table. We must create conditions in which people want to be led. We cannot lead people from here to there if they have not first been welcomed *here*.

Leaders must work hard to engage people at the level of their will. The people we are trying to influence can, except in rare circumstances, do whatever they please. We are wise if we create pleasing environments where they are more willing to do the good things we are attempting to lead them to do. Biographer Jean Edward Smith recounts an incident during the Second World War when General George Marshall was resistant to a military action President Franklin Roosevelt wanted taken. Roosevelt, America's longest serving president, had an instinctive awareness of what the American people wanted. Though he ultimately would make decisions based on what he believed was in the best interests of those he led—as any leader should—he knew that if he paid attention to public opinion and led in tandem with the will of the people, his decisions would bring a better result. The president pushed General Marshall to take action that he believed Americans would support, as opposed to the strategy Marshall wanted to pursue from a purely military perspective. Roosevelt prevailed, the action was taken, and the results were effective and historic. Much later, General Marshall confessed that he had in fact been wrong in his leadership approach. With new insight he said, "We failed to see that the leader in a democracy has to keep the people entertained."

In ways obvious and subtle, hospitable leaders "entertain" those we lead—or want to lead. It is simply easier to influence people who have been welcomed to the table. A famous example of this is when Jesus fed the five thousand. You know the story: Jesus was in a town on the shore of the Sea of Galilee, and a huge crowd came to see Him. He welcomed them. Jesus was concerned that they didn't have anything to eat. He took a little bit of food, enough for one little boy, and multiplied it into a whole lot of food—enough for more than five thousand people. Characteristic of the hospitality of Jesus, there were even leftovers.

It is simply easier to influence people who have been welcomed to the table.

That night Jesus got into a boat with His disciples (actually walked on the water to the boat) and sailed to another town on the Galilean shore. The next morning the crowd "realized that neither Jesus nor his disciples were there, [and] they got into the boats and went in search of Jesus."

Note, they went searching for Him. You know you are leading well when people are searching for you! When they found Him, Jesus told them He knew they were only looking for Him because they knew He could feed them. But now that they were there, He could talk about what He really wanted to talk about: "Do not work for food that spoils, but for food that endures to eternal life." He then announced that He was the bread of life and that whoever believed in Him would never be hungry again.

The meal he fed the five thousand was more than a meal; it was not really about the fish and bread. I have no doubt that Jesus was terribly concerned about the physical hunger of the people. He was hospitable in their need. But with Jesus, dinner was usually about more than dinner. Now that He had their attention, He could lead them to more than they knew they needed. He could say what really needed to be said. He could exercise influence.

The people could have gone wherever they wanted to that morning. But because he had "entertained" them, they were engaged at the level of their will. And they went looking for Him. Now He could offer them something more than breakfast—he could offer them the Bread of Life.

Hospitality provided a pathway for Jesus to move His mission forward, and to offer the people more than they had ever dreamed of. Hospitality creates environments for people and dreams to flourish.

From a business perspective, Starbucks founder Howard Schultz articulates some aspects of hospitable leadership as well as anyone. He understands the importance of creating environments in which people can be led to make decisions aligned with organizational objectives. In his case, that's to buy coffee, of course. "The merchant's success depends on his or her ability to tell a story. What people see or hear or smell or do when they enter a space guides their feelings, enticing them to celebrate whatever the seller has to offer."

I was talking to a small-business owner recently who was asking me about hospitable leadership. She seemed dubious that it would matter to her bottom line. This was an easy one for me. I explained to her what should be obvious to us all. When people engage your business, they either feel invited or they don't. They sense welcome or they don't. They intuit this when they navigate your website. They perceive it when they see your signage. They know it when they walk through the front door. The physical space speaks to them. The receptionist usually confirms impressions already made. And here's the deal: It's difficult to sell your services to someone who doesn't feel welcomed. You must get people to the table in order to influence them. When people experience hospitality—when they are enticed—they are more inclined to say yes to what you have to offer.

As Schultz writes,

> Ideally, every Starbucks store should tell a story about coffee and what we as an organization believe in. That story should unfold via the taste and presentation of our products as well as the sights, sounds, and smells that surround our customers. The aroma of freshly ground coffee. Interior hues, textures, the shapes and materials of furniture and fixtures, as well as their origins. The art on the walls. The music. The rhythm of the coffee bar and how our partners move and speak behind the counter. . . . Each store's ambiance is the manifestation of a larger purpose, and at Starbucks each shop's multidimensional sensory experiences has always defined our brand.

Every leader who wants to accomplish good purposes must be aware of what the climate of the organization we serve is saying. Though words are part of this environmental reality, sometimes the overall atmospherics of a place speak so loudly that people can't hear what we actually want to say.

This attention to hospitality is not only for our customers; it is even more important for our employees or teams. Ken Gosnell blogged that "business owners need to view their business as a home and their employees as guests on a regular basis." I like that he didn't say to treat employees like family. Sadly, we are often more hospitable to guests than we are to our families. We should treat our employees as guests.

This has been a paradigm-shifting challenge for me. Am I hospitable to the people who work with me? Who show up every day and partner with me to accomplish our shared vision? I desperately hope so. I hope this is reflected in the office space we carefully designed—full of light, inviting, warm. I hope this is reflected in hospitable policies and internal communications and how performance is measured and rewarded, and even how team members transition off of our team if and when that time comes. I hope this is reflected in the hundreds of simple interactions that occur as the days fly by—through kind words, by trying to catch people doing something right, in finding any possible excuse to praise them. And with simple courtesies such as *please* and *thank you* and *my pleasure* and *you're welcome*. I've not always been successful at this. I have learned. I am learning. I do know that when I create an environment of welcome for those who work with me, they will give me permission to lead them to do great things.

Some time ago I met a guy named Paul Theodore as I was greeting people in the lobby after the Sunday service. He mentioned he was a partner in a sign company. Only later—as I got to know him better—did I discover that it's not your average sign company. Paul is the president and CEO of Visual Graphic Systems, Inc. If you walk into any Starbucks in the world, you see menu signage that Visual Graphic designed or manufactured. Same at Subway, Kentucky Fried Chicken, Taco Bell, Dunkin' Donuts, and any number of other fast-food franchises. If you visit the Museum of Modern Art, or the Lincoln

Center in New York City, or Yale University in New Haven, Connecticut, you see VGS's sign systems. If you see the famous bow and ribbon across the landmarked Cartier building during a magical Manhattan Christmas, think VGS. And those are just *some* of the things they do.

Paul is one of four partners at VGS. At least for now. As I was writing this chapter, I bumped into Paul and asked him how he was doing. He said he was a little stressed, that he's been working a lot of extra hours. I asked him if something unusual was going on. He said yes; he and his partners have decided to share ownership of a large percentage of their company with their employees, approximately 125 of them. My interest was piqued. "Why are you doing that?" I asked. He explained that VGS has doubled its revenue in the past five or six years and is growing rapidly. Part of this growth necessitated moving out of Manhattan to Carlstadt, New Jersey. This meant that most of his employees, many of whom have been with the company for many years, are commuting from one of the five New York City boroughs. This has impacted the quality of their lives, and he has been concerned that too many of them are living paycheck to paycheck and having trouble saving for retirement. So he and his partners decided to divide a significant percentage of the company into stock that will be paid into their employees'—now owners'—retirement accounts. Paul is excited because if the company is ever sold, people will not lose their jobs but rather be enriched. Everybody in the company will win. The company is owned by its employees, after all.

There's also this: Paul dreams of continuing to grow the company and serving his customers ever better. He knows that owners will be motivated to work hard and long to grow *their* company. Paul understands that moral leaders do not have to choose between caring for people and working toward the fulfillment of their own dreams. They can do both at the same time. Hospitable leaders create environments where people and dreams flourish.

It boggles my mind to see how applicable the leadership practices of Jesus are to this discussion. At the Last Supper, Jesus demonstrated a blend of hospitality and leadership that is breathtaking. He created an environment where He modeled leadership at its very best, and led a leadership discussion that empowered His followers to change the world forever.

It began when He ensured the preparation of the physical space where the Last Supper was to be held. Luke puts it like this in his gospel:

> Jesus sent Peter and John, saying, "Go and make preparations for us to eat the Passover." "Where do you want us to prepare for it?" they asked. He replied, "As you enter the city, a man carrying a jar of water will meet you. Follow him to the house that he enters, and say to the owner of the house, 'The Teacher asks: Where is the guest room, where I may eat the Passover with my disciples?' He will show you a large room upstairs, all furnished. Make preparations there." They left and found things just as Jesus had told them. So they prepared the Passover."

This provision is often overlooked in the story of the Last Supper. And in discussions about leadership. Jesus ensured that His last dinner with His disciples would be held in a hospitable environment. He made certain that the room was large enough and adequately furnished. He instructed Peter and John to make preparations for the Passover dinner in that space—no doubt a meticulous and time-consuming task. A lamb slain. Wine purchased. A table set for twelve plus one.

When His guests arrived, Jesus set the spiritual climate in a way that reflected the importance of this dinner. John said, in his gospel, that in this moment, Jesus showed the "full extent of his love." The air must have been heavy with emotion. I don't know what He said to convey that much passion, but He didn't need to say much. The atmosphere was thick with love.

Then, in the greatest act of servant leadership ever recorded, "he got up from the meal, took off his outer clothing, and wrapped a towel around his waist. After that, he poured water into a basin and began to wash his disciples' feet, drying them with the towel that was wrapped around him." He assumed the position of the lowest of servants. He did what perhaps someone else in the room should have offered to do. He washed the dirty feet of His followers. I love the words that precede this act: "Jesus knew that the Father had put all things under his power, and that he had come from God and was returning to God." I like to say, and will say, that hospitable leadership at its zenith is a state of being. It flows out of who we are. Jesus could serve His followers in this way because He knew who He was. And because He knew who He was, He could selflessly show them how much He cared for them.

> **Jesus demonstrated a blend of hospitality and leadership that is breathtaking.**

You have to imagine that His disciples hung on every word Jesus uttered in that environment. As they ate and drank, and then finally walked together to Gethsemane on that fateful night, Jesus gave a leadership talk for the ages. He cast vision for their shared future. He engaged in the most extreme team building, commanding them to love one another, even to the point of laying down their lives for each other. He prayed passionately for unity. He gave them buy-in, if you please, to His Father's business, saying, "I no longer call you servants, because a servant does not know his master's business. Instead, I have called you friends, for everything that I learned from my Father

I have made known to you." He established expectations and let them know He would be measuring results: "I chose you and appointed you so that you might go and bear fruit—fruit that will last." He expected them to produce!

All this leadership activity happened in the context of hospitality. You can't practice servant leadership unless you have welcomed people in. Hospitable leaders create space physically, spiritually, emotionally, and relationally where all other forms of moral leadership can be employed.

***

Jon Meacham wrote a beautiful book in which he painted an intimate portrait of the epic friendship between Franklin Delano Roosevelt and Winston Churchill. He eloquently makes the point that they were not just friends, but that their relationship was about something bigger than their bond. As the primary leaders of the free world, they each felt destined to save humanity from Hitler and the other Axis powers. "A friendship like Roosevelt and Churchill's is rightly understood as a fond relationship in which two people have an interest not just in each other (though they do) but also, as [Ralph Waldo] Emerson saw, in a shared external truth or mission." Meacham wrote that "C. S. Lewis noted that Emerson once observed, *Do you love me?* actually means *Do you see the same truth?* Or at least . . . Do you *care about* the same truth?"

Meacham's insight helps make the point that this book is not just another book about hospitality, at least not primarily. It is about hospitable *leadership*. Roosevelt and Churchill didn't just enjoy having dinner together. They had dinner together around a common purpose. Together, they were trying to save the world.

Leaders have a job to do. In our own way, we each have a world to save. Pastors, moms, teachers—and CEOs responsible for the livelihoods of a whole lot of people. Hospitality is good in and of itself. But I want us to see the potential of hospitality to create a platform to engage people—to lead people from where they are to where they should be.

This does not mean that hospitable leadership is utilitarian, a Machiavellian means to an end. That would not be hospitable. Practicing leadership with a hospitality mindset is the right way—the moral way—to lead people. It is community with purpose, fellowship with outcomes, hospitality with results.

The earliest leaders of the Christian church devoted themselves to "teaching and to fellowship, to the breaking of bread and to prayer," and "the Lord added to their number daily." Something more than fellowship came out of their fellowship. The requirement for early church leaders to be hospitable wasn't so they could just hang out. They had a mission to accomplish. And accomplish it they did.

Practicing leadership with a hospitality mindset is the right way—the moral way—to lead people.

When I see Jesus sitting in the middle of a great feast, looking at me and inviting me in, I know He is inviting me to eat with Him, to fellowship with Him, and I thrill to that. But I know that's not all that's going on. I also know He is inviting me to join Him in what He is doing. He is creating space where I can flourish—where dreams come true. That's what hospitable leaders do. I want to be a leader like that.

Leadership Take-Homes

1. **Create environments that feel like warm, welcoming feasts.**
   Hospitality provided the pathway for Jesus to advance His

mission; to advance ours, we must earnestly embrace His hospitable example.

2. **Create environments where people want to be led, and engage them at the level of their will.** It is easier to influence people who have been invited in and welcomed to the table.

3. **Identify the physical, emotional, and relational pathways leading to your goals.** When Jesus fed the five thousand, He wasn't simply providing a meal, but offering an accessible path to the core of His message.

Sources

"What Jesus did here in Cana of Galilee": John 2:11.

He described His kingdom as a wedding: Matthew 22:2 NIV.

"the Son of Man came": Tim Chester, *A Meal with Jesus: Discovering Grace, Community, and Mission around the Table* (Wheaton, IL: Crossway, 2011), 12.

"to seek and to save the lost": Luke 19:10.

"to serve others and to give": Mark 10:45 NLT.

"The Son of Man came eating": Luke 7:34.

"We failed to see that the leader": Jean Edward Smith, *Eisenhower: In War and Peace* (New York: Random House, 2012), 216.

"realized that neither Jesus nor his disciples": John 6:24.

"Do not work for food that spoils": John 6:27.

"The merchant's success depends on his or her ability.": Howard Schultz, *Onward: How Starbucks Fought for Its Life without Losing Its Soul* (New York: Rodale, 2011), 34.

"Ideally, every Starbucks store should tell a story": Schultz, *Onward*, 273–274.

"business owners need to view their business": Ken Gosnell, "The Secret Leadership Traits—HOSPITABLE," December 3, 2015, Linkedin.com.

"Jesus sent Peter and John": Luke 22:8–13.

"the full extent of his love": John 13:1 NLT, note.

"he got up from the meal": John 13:4–5.

"Jesus knew that the Father had": John 13:3.

"I no longer call you servants": John 15:15.

"I chose you and appointed you": John 15:16.

"A friendship like Roosevelt and Churchill's": Jon Meacham, *Franklin and Winston: An Intimate Portrait of an Epic Friendship* (New York: Random House, 2004), xvii.

"C.S. Lewis noted that Emerson once observed": Meacham, *Franklin and Winston*, xvii.

"devoted themselves to teaching": Acts 2:42, 47.

2

The Power of a Warm Heart

I love Andrei Kravchuk's 2005 film *The Italian*. In this beautiful work we are introduced to Vanya Solntsev. This six-year-old boy—apparently orphaned—is forced to endure the most severe deprivations of a Russian orphanage run by an alcoholic and corrupt headmaster. It appears he was rescued forever when a wealthy young Italian couple arrive to adopt a child. They choose Vanya and make plans to take him back to Italy for a life of luxury beyond his wildest dreams. Italy! Just the name of the place sounds like magic. His envious friends begin to call him "the Italian."

And then Vanya discovers that his mother is still alive. He is heartsick that she might return to reclaim him only to discover he has been adopted. So he breaks into the headmaster's office, finds his file, and learns his mother's address. He escapes the orphanage and embarks on a dangerous mission to find her. Italy may sound magical, but it is not home, and Vanya is willing to risk everything to find *home*. The film closes with Vanya reunited with his mother. Her home is aesthetically unattractive.

But his reunion with her is beautiful beyond aesthetics. He is home.

After some time he writes to Anton, his friend from the orphanage who has been adopted by the Italian couple in Vanya's place. "Hello, Anton," he writes. "Thank you for your letter. I didn't know oranges grew where you live. Here it rains all the time, but it's warm inside."

It is nearly impossible to describe the allure of home. I feel home, though, as I read Vanya's words. Home is where our heart is warm regardless of what is going on outside.

If you have a good and happy home, you understand exactly what I mean. If you have not experienced such a home, you understand what I mean as well; you are lonely for a home like that.

Most of us spend much of our life trying to get home . . . wherever home is. Before I was married, home was wherever my parents were. But for the last thirty-five years, home is wherever Sharon, my wife, is. Wherever we are, if Sharon is there, I am home.

Hospitable leaders embrace the mystery of home. We are aware of the need every human being has to be embraced in its inexplicable warmth. I want the people I attempt to lead to feel home in the climate I create with my presence, in the midst of my efforts to influence them, and in every nuance of my communications with them. A leader who connects to the subconscious need in each of us for the warmth of home is one who cultivates environments where people and dreams—the dreams of the followers and the leader—can flourish. This is not sentimentality. Fostering environments that say "home" in most every leadership sphere makes room for leadership to be more effective. It creates space where relationships can be nurtured around purpose, where the trust necessary for synergistic accomplishment is engendered, and where truth can be spoken in a way it will actually be received.

Jesus made a connection with people on a warm heart level that allowed Him to say and do things that were received in a way never witnessed before. Put simply, people felt at home with Jesus. And they were willing to follow Him anywhere.

Remember the story of Jesus joining the disciples on the road to Emmaus? These two were discussing the "rumors" of Jesus' resurrection when He came up and started walking with them. He didn't allow them to recognize Him at first. But while they ate dinner together, their eyes were opened to who He was. And after He disappeared, they realized that they had, in fact, been aware of something very familiar in His presence. They asked each other, "Were not our hearts burning within us while he talked with us on the road and opened the Scriptures to us?" It's as if they said, "Oh yeah, we should've known that was him. . . . We have felt that before. Our hearts are always warm when we are with him."

> **A leader who connects to the subconscious need in each of us for the warmth of home is one who cultivates environments where people and dreams can flourish.**

In her fifteenth-century spiritual classic *The Showings of Divine Love*, Julian of Norwich referred to Jesus as "homely." She did not mean he was ugly, of course. In the Middle English vernacular in which she wrote, *homely* referred to "friendliness." Julian was saying that in her profound vision of Jesus, she felt welcomed—invited in. She was home. I want to be a homely leader. When people are with me, I want their hearts to be warmed. If I am to lead them somewhere, I believe home is a good place to begin that journey.

You may rightfully ask, "What in the world does this have to do with leadership?" Fair question. A leader who can warm people's hearts can lead them to more. Abraham Lincoln said that "in order to 'win a man to your cause' . . . you must first reach his heart, 'the great high road to his reason.'" I have learned over many years of leadership that if I can warm people's hearts, I can lead them to most any good thing.

I do not believe there is a class in any business school called "How to Warm Hearts." But maybe there should be. For whatever reason—perhaps our proximity to New York City and Wall Street—I am surrounded by people with MBAs, MOLs, PhDs, and other advanced training in sciences such as business management and organizational leadership. A number of them have been educated in the top business schools in the world. I am always honored when these leaders are eager to hear me teach about leadership . . . but at times, frankly, I wonder why. I am aware that when I teach about the more technical aspects of leadership, I probably seldom say anything that these accomplished men and women haven't already heard. Even though I too have been formally educated in the discipline of organizational leadership, many of the people I speak to could teach me more than I could ever teach them about any number of leadership activities. Like how to develop a strategic plan, for instance.

That is not the unique strength I bring to the leadership discussion. Nor is it the reason I have written this book. I have come to understand that these leaders respond to me because I am somehow able to communicate about the enigmatic qualities of leadership that give life to some otherwise sterile leadership practice. I specialize in warming hearts. Strategic planning—and every other leadership practice—is infinitely more effective when people's hearts are warmed.

I have sat in far too many strategic planning sessions where I just wished I could lie down on the floor and go to sleep. Maybe forever. But I have also been in many planning sessions—and led them—where the atmosphere was pregnant with destiny, where there was a sense of God's very presence, an ineffable joy, an awareness of near-limitless possibility. Not only did I not want to nod off, but I could hardly sleep for days after because I was so excited with potentiality.

My guess is that you know just what I mean. Sometimes this has to do with the nature of what is being planned, I suppose. But let's assume the "I'm wide awake" session and the "I just want to go to sleep" session are about the same positive thing. A leader must work to create environmental conditions that warm hearts.

How often I have coached a sincere and highly credentialed leader after they led a meeting about something that should have had everyone fired up and ready to go, but instead was just another boring meeting. I ask them the most simple—even obvious—questions. Did you fire up your heart as a part of your preparation? Did you convey that passion in a way that caused people to feel your heart? Did you connect this meeting to compelling vision? If not, why did we have it? Did you think through how to help the participants engage with one another in ways that would help them know each other better and facilitate them being unified in your common cause? Did you plan fun? And so on.

I have observed that many times when a high-stakes meeting is flat, the results are flat. Why? Because every person needs to come away from a meeting like that not only with knowledge and goals and action items, but also with the passion and will to do the work. This is a matter of the heart, not the mind.

We must pay attention to the soft side of leadership if we want hard results. Many leaders are most focused on the information to be shared. They spend their time preparing charts and PowerPoint presentations. They are "let's get down to business, just the facts, ma'am" Joe Fridays. And they miss people's hearts. We need to spend time planning appropriate humor—framing every "we've got to get better" in positive ways—and sharing heartwarming stories of how what we are doing is changing people's lives. We must do much more than transmit information. We must impart purpose, desire, love.

Then, of course, there is the preparation of physical space. When people walk into a room, they sense whether or not we have been planning for them. On some level this signals whether or not we care about them. Hospitably presented food and drink warm the heart. I can't imagine Jesus having significant meetings with no attention paid to the meal. And then—if we are smart—we ensure there is an inspiring setting and comfortable seating that helps create the conditions for effective communication.

Some of the most memorable meetings I have led over the years have been in our home where we lavished our teammates with hospitality, or in nature, or anchored on a boat in the middle of a lake, or in some beautiful rented space like a fabulous mansion someone let us use for a staff team retreat. It is worth the effort—and when possible, the money—to create the conditions to really engage people's hearts, especially in those pivotal moments when the discussions are laden with destiny and future-shaping possibilities.

We took great care when we designed our present offices to have spacious meeting rooms with invigorating views, comfortable seating, and the obligatory technological bells and whistles. But you can grab people's hearts in the simplest environments. I am thinking about a meeting I led some twenty-five years ago in a darkish, musty Sunday school room in the basement of an ancient church our young congregation was renting at that time. About ten of us were packed in that room sitting around a table, as I remember it. We were having a planning session about the small groups we were about to launch for the first time in our young history. I was passionate about this and was attempting to share my vision of how this would serve so many people so well. I got so fired up, I jumped up on the table and paced back and forth, pouring my heart out like so much molten lava.

Twenty-five years later, people still talk about that meeting. "Do you remember that day you jumped up on the table . . . ?" I do not jump up on tables anymore. At least not physically. But I still feel that same passion and I work hard to make sure the people I lead feel my heart burn at every appropriate opportunity. And most of the time, their hearts get warm too. When their hearts warm up, they don't just stay awake . . . they come alive. They open to possibility. They engage their hearts in our mission. Then all my other leadership efforts become an experience, not just some boring process. Hospitable leaders are experts in warming hearts.

Our statement of values at The Life Christian Church is called *The TLCC Way*. One of our values is, "We are always hospitable." I know there is nothing particularly unique about an organizational value of hospitality. But one of the sub-points to this value is, "We massage people's hearts." I love it. So let's say the leader of the "better than Starbucks" Life Café in our lobby is training her team. She will teach them that we are not just serving a cappuccino to our guests—we are massaging their hearts. We are not in the coffee business; we are in the heart business. We serve a warm drink in a way that warms hearts.

Our hope is that the lobby looks great, the signage communicates clearly, and the line moves quickly. Nothing freezes the heart like a long wait to be served! We should interact with the guest using hospitable language like, "How may I serve you?" and "My pleasure." But more than this is the heart engagement. This is the mystery of it all. The team member must care about the person they are serving. They must pay attention to the experience beyond whatever item has been ordered. They must serve the customer with an understanding of our larger purpose. The guest must feel home.

In many cases, that guest will walk from the Life Café to the auditorium to hear someone, like me, share truths that should be transformative. I want to teach people with warm hearts.

So in this and many other ways more explicitly spiritual and important, we aspire to massage people's hearts.

———

The president of Pixar and Disney animation, Edwin Catmull, captured some of the idea of home in the work environment when he wrote about the Steve Jobs–designed Pixar campus in San Francisco. The site was fashioned so people would be encouraged to "mingle, meet and communicate." Catmull wrote further that though the building is luxurious, that isn't the point. It was built for community. The experience of a guest walking into Pixar "leaves them feeling a little wistful, like something is missing in their work lives—a palpable energy, a feeling of collaboration and unfettered creativity, a sense, not to be corny, of possibility."

This is what a well-thought-through environment can do, whether physical or immaterial. Somehow it incites possibility. Brené Brown referred to a teacher who wrote to her and said, "For me, teaching is about love. It is not about transferring information, but rather creating an atmosphere of mystery and imagination and discovery." That's great! This teacher gets "home." This is more than teaching to a test; it's uncovering the innate desire children have to learn. Sadly, there are some who think this kind of sentiment has nothing to do with teaching. But most of us know better.

Sharon homeschooled all three of our now-adult children. Each of them—Sumerr, Caleb, and Christian—love to read, learn, and grow. Sharon is not a formally trained teacher, just a mom who loves her kids and created an environment in the home where each child could learn in his or her own way. It almost seems unfair. While many of their peers were on a school bus early in the morning and spending the day in a structured institutional environment, our kids would be wherever they were most comfortable in our home, learning in a way that matched who they were as individuals. They learned to love to read the classics and visit museums—to which they drag me to this day—and have conversations about what they were learning with adults. Each of them went to public schools when they were older, excelled in that environment as well, did great on standardized tests, and were accepted into great colleges. But their love for learning was initially stimulated in the home. Our home was an environment where the natural desire to learn was nurtured in our kids.

My wife is a hospitable leader. In her case, this is not about technique as much as it is about creating an environment where an individual opens to possibility. She has always felt inferior to other educators, though. A validating moment for her came when Caleb, our middle child, was interviewed by the dean of admissions at Yale University on the weekend they offered him a football scholarship. They were a little concerned that this kid, who had been educated by his mom until he was a freshman in high school, might not be able to survive the elite educational challenge of an Ivy League school. After the interview, the dean sought Sharon out. She said, "I just want to meet the woman who homeschooled this amazing young man."

We regularly hear similar things from a variety of people about each of our kids. They are far from perfect, of course, but they are each, in their own way, big inside, with their eyes wide open to a world full of possibility. I know I sound like a doting dad here—and I am!—but I am attempting to make a larger point. Many people, including West Orange Public School teachers, church leaders, and others, have served our children so well. But our children's success began in a home with a mom who created an environment that encouraged their love of learning and exploring God's dreams for their lives.

Obviously, everyone can't—or even shouldn't—homeschool their children. But I have seen teachers in even the most challenging school districts create "home" in their classrooms. Carl

Brister was a public school teacher in Orange, New Jersey, when he wrote me an email detailing how he changed his approach in his classroom in response to hearing me teach about hospitable leadership. "Over the years I've seen quite a bit from school-wide lock-downs to intruders with guns, to mice running thru the class during the lesson. This year in particular I was transferred to a school where 94 percent of the students failed math the previous year and were at least two to three grade levels behind. . . . It's been a battle since day one." But then Carl decided to change the environment in a most difficult educational setting. "Now, as a result of my switch to a hospitable leadership style in the classroom, many of my students have shown tremendous growth and are surpassing math goals and learning targets, and meeting grade-level benchmarks."

A hospitable leader creates home wherever he or she is. Many of us lead in inhospitable places. We must be thermostats, not thermometers. We must set the temperature for success. Artist and mystic Hazrat Inayat Khan reminds us that "some people look for a beautiful place, others make a place beautiful." Hospitable leaders bring the beauty of home to even the most inhospitable places.

We become who we are in the environment of home. We are shaped by our families. Home is formative. Sociologist Cody C. Delistraty explored the most recent scientific literature for *Atlantic Monthly* and discovered that the single most important element in raising kids who are drug-free, healthy, intelligent, kind human beings is frequent family dinners. The most important predictor of success for elementary-aged children is frequent family dinners. The primary factor in shaping vocabulary for younger children is frequent family dinners. The key variable most associated with a lower incidence of depressive and suicidal thoughts among eleven- to eighteen-year-olds is frequent family dinners.

There is something quasi-sacramental about the table—any table where an environment of home is created. A sacrament is a physical thing in which God—or something of God—is seen and is present. Without question, some of the most sacred moments of my life have been experienced sitting at the dinner table with my wife and kids. Of lesser importance, but still extremely significant: I've had many experiences sitting at the table with members

> **A hospitable leader creates home wherever he or she is.**

of my team when something of God and eternity has broken into our bread breaking. I've seen conference tables in hospitable environments become the Lord's table. A means of grace. As N. T. Wright wrote, "When Jesus himself wanted to explain to his disciples what his forthcoming death was all about, he didn't give them a theory, he gave them a meal."

I encourage leaders to see hospitality as formative. As something uniquely important that God can use. That just as surely as the dinner table is essential for a family to shape a child, so any leader should see hospitality as a means to shape people's lives and help them grow and flourish and move an organization's mission forward.

Michael Frost intimates that there are certain environments where the imagined veil that separates heaven from earth is "thin": "The Celts speak of 'thin places,' where the fabric that separates heaven and earth is so thin it becomes almost translucent and one is able to encounter the joy and peace of heaven." Theologian Barry Jones responded to Frost by writing that "for me the veil is thin when I'm seated at the table with good food and cherished friends." I agree.

Hospitable leaders are intentional about creating environments where the veil is thin. One of the most memorable family meals I can remember happened on the weekend Christian, our youngest, graduated from Wheaton College in Illinois. We reserved a special place to have breakfast together for our family of five and my mom and dad. We ate breakfast for more than three hours. We kept ordering food because we didn't want to leave the table. We laughed and told stories and lingered in the presence of family. And God. The veil was thin. Something of God breaks into moments like this.

Somehow, I know I need to figure out ways to replicate these kinds of experiences in each of my leadership domains. It doesn't have to be a meal—just unhurried time when we are together in settings where we feel home.

To offer home we must be at home. This is not primarily a physical place or set of practices. Home is a state of being. Home is the spirit of a person. Or an organization. The hospitality that warms people's hearts must flow out of warm hearts.

This is so important: Hospitality that does not flow from the heart is not hospitality at all. People quickly detect a superficial niceness—a practiced technique, an inauthentic perfection. We do not need to be Martha Stewart or the Marriott to welcome people into our home or organization. It would be nice to set a table like Martha or to train our teams like the Marriott does. We should care about presentation and practice a lot. But a home filled with love and warmth is magic whether the table is set perfectly or not. In fact, aiming for perfection seems to mess something up in the heart of the host. It often keeps us from simply and excitedly offering genuine hospitality. And an organization—school, business, church—that focuses first on techniques rather than the interior condition of its people is missing something as well. When we focus first on engaging the heart, we touch that part of a person that is lonely for home.

When someone is at home, the practice of hospitality seems effortless—natural, fluid, real. Tolstoy wrote that every good host tries to make his guests feel "that everything that is so well arranged at his host's has not cost him, the host, any effort at all but has come about of itself." This is what happens when thoughtful hospitality techniques flow out of a hospitable state of being. Guests do not notice what they see and hear as much as they notice what they feel. They feel at home.

The good news—literally—is that Jesus offers each of us the state of being called home. At the Last Supper He told His disciples that He was going home to His Father and that they would be able to join Him there. "There is more than enough room in my Father's home. . . . When everything is ready, I will come and get you, so that you will always be with me where I am. And you know the way to where I am going. . . . I am the way, the truth, and the life."

> When someone is at home, the practice of hospitality seems effortless— natural, fluid, real.

Jesus was saying that He was about to go home to His Father and that there was room in His home for each of them. He was not talking exclusively—or even primarily—about His eternal home. He was promising them that God's home was about to break into the present reality of their lives. He went on to tell them that from His home, He would make His home *in* them. "I will not abandon you as orphans—I will come to you. . . . When I am raised to life again, you will know that I am in my Father, and you are in me, and I am in you." He would live in them. They would live in Him. The resulting state is a condition called home. He made it clear that home was not something that only they would experience, but that anyone who believed in Him and followed Him could experience. There is enough room in His Father's home for everyone.

Let me put it like this: If we are in relationship with Jesus, we are in a state of being called home. And the more we cultivate our relationship with Jesus, the more at home we become.

I know many people who I would call hospitable leaders. Leaders from whom I have learned much. Many of them follow Jesus. Some do not. Part of hospitality lives in the realm of common grace, our common humanity rooted in the fact that we are all created in the image of God. I have no doubt, however, that any one of us could be a more hospitable leader if we followed Jesus and grew in relationship with Him. He is the most hospitable leader who has ever lived, or does live. And He promised that if we believe in Him, He is at home in us and we are at home in Him.

Without qualification, the single most important dimension of my leadership experience is my relationship with Jesus. Sadly, by my very nature, I am not given to hospitality. But like those guys on the road to Emmaus two thousand years ago, I know my heart has grown warmer and warmer and warmer as I have walked with Jesus over many years. I am home. And I am more at home every day. This gives me hope that anyone—including me—can truly be a hospitable leader.

Leadership Take-Homes

1. **Embrace the mystery of home.** Many people spend their entire lives searching for a sense of belonging. If you offer this, you offer everything.

2. **Create the conditions that warm hearts.** Every leadership practice is infinitely more effective when people's hearts are warmed.

3. **To offer home we must be at home.** True hospitality is achieved not by perfection of place, but in the power of genuine warmth and love. Jesus offers each of us that state called home with and in Him.

Sources

"Hello, Anton": *The Italian*, Andrei Kravchuk, dir., film, Russia (Sony Pictures, 2005).

"Were not our hearts burning within us": Luke 24:32.

"homely" . . . **"friendliness"**: Julian of Norwich, *The Showings of Julian of Norwich*, trans., Mirabai Starr (Charlottesville: Hampton, 2013), xxi.

"win a man to your cause": Doris Kearns Goodwin, *The Political Genius of Abraham Lincoln* (New York: Simon & Schuster, 2005), 168.

"mingle, meet and communicate.": Edwin Catmull, *Creativity, Inc.: Overcoming the Unseen Forces That Stand in the Way of True Inspiration* (New York: Random House, 2014), x, ix.

"For me, teaching is about love.": Brené Brown, *Daring Greatly* (New York: Avery-Imprint Penguin-Random House, 2012), 136.

"Over the years I've seen": Carl Brister, email communication with Terry Smith, February 19, 2017.

"the single most important element in raising kids": Leonard Sweet, *From Tablet to Table* (Colorado Springs: NavPress, 2014), 9–12.

"When Jesus himself wanted to explain to his disciples": Barry Jones, *Dwell: Life with God for the World* (Downers Grove: InterVarsity Press, 2014), 180.

"The Celts speak of 'thin places'": Barry Jones, *Dwell: Life with God for the World*, 180.

"that everything that is so well arranged": Leo Tolstoy, *Anna Karenina* (New York: Bantam, 1981), 753.

"There is more than enough room": John 14:2–4, 6 NLT.

"I will not abandon you as orphans": John 14:18, 20 NLT.

Welcome Two

STRANGERS

3

Stranger Angels

Thankfully, on the trip to Paris I mentioned earlier, we did not just visit museums. We also enjoyed some wonderful meals—including a very memorable dinner at the Eiffel Tower Terrace Restaurant. The previous week, France had suffered a series of terrible terrorist attacks. The Eiffel Tower was actually closed a couple of days before our arrival because of the heightened threat level. So even as we savored an excellently prepared French meal on a perfect Parisian summer evening, the air was heavy with potential danger.

After our meal, Caleb ordered an Uber on his phone. We stood on the street facing the Eiffel Tower with thousands of people from all over the world milling around on the street, sidewalks, and courtyard leading to and surrounding the tower. I was thrilled to be in the middle of it all and wasn't paying any attention to what I later learned was some confusion around trying to secure our Uber ride. All I knew was that after several minutes, Sharon said, "There's our Uber. Let's go." I turned around, and she and Caleb were already jumping into the car—Caleb in the front passenger seat and Sharon in the seat behind him. I caught up quickly and jerked open the door to get in—street side, behind the driver. But as I did, Sharon and Caleb were getting out and shouting to me, "Get out! Get out!" I wasn't even in all the way yet, but I got out fast! The car took off, tires screeching and siren blaring. Wait . . . siren? "What happened?" I asked.

Excitedly, nervously, they told me that as they opened their doors and got in, Caleb asked the driver, "Are you our Uber?" The driver looked at him and smiled, saying, "No, I'm this." He reached under his seat, grabbed a big, blue siren, and placed it on the dashboard. Oops. The guy we thought was our Uber driver was an undercover cop, evidently in the midst of responding to a dangerous threat. Sirens were screaming all over by then as a number of police cars rushed to face whatever menace threatened the city.

Here's what struck me in that moment: So this French policeman, in the middle of a city on high alert and on the verge of police action in the epicenter of terrorist activity in Europe, somehow assumed the best about the strangers who unexpectedly piled into his car on that Paris street. My son is a good-looking kid, but physically imposing, a big guy and former football tight end. As an actor, he recently had played a bad guy on an episode of *Agents of Shield*, and he played the part well. The response of this policeman could have been dramatically different. We laugh about this story now of course, but it could have had a terribly different ending.

At some point it occurred to me how different our world would be if each of us assumed the best when we encountered a stranger, or even when a stranger imposed themselves on us in some strange way. Especially when our background and experiences might give us cause to be angry or afraid and to react in a negative way. Obviously, we need to be careful and cautious about terrorist threats and other extreme potentialities— I'm not referring to that kind of thing. I mean the multitude of encounters we have with people who are not like us, or are not familiar to us. People who, in our societal climate, might even arouse suspicion. Those we might instinctually keep at a distance and feel the need to protect ourselves from. Strangers. The author of the New Testament letter to the Hebrews taught us that we must "Remember to welcome strangers, because some who have done this have welcomed angels without knowing it," or "Do not forget to show hospitality to strangers, for by so doing some people have shown hospitality to angels without knowing it."

A stranger, for the purpose of this discussion, is anyone who seems strange to you. Or to whom you may seem strange. This could be someone you do not know or who does not know you, whose background, worldview, or lifestyle may seem strange to you. A stranger could also be someone you do know but who is from a different nation of origin, race, or ethnicity. Or someone from a different socioeconomic or educational status. Or someone who has different political views or a different faith experience than you.

In another way, a stranger could be—and surely is in some ways—your spouse. Even though you know them intimately, you may sometimes feel like you don't know them at all. After all, as the Bible says, men are from Mars, women are from Venus. Or maybe that was John Gray.

In some seasons of life, a stranger could even be your child. Or a patient, student, employee, or perhaps even a congregant. Anyone you feel is—even just sometimes—strange to you.

I like the progression of this passage in Hebrews 13: first, we are to "Keep on loving each other as brothers and sisters." This phrase has its etymology in the Greek word *philadelphia*, which is also translated famously as "brotherly love." Second, we are reminded to "not forget to show hospitality to strangers." This phrase comes from the Greek *philoxenia*, which literally means "love of strangers." According to Scripture (and Google Maps,

I think), we must go through Philadelphia in order to arrive in Philoxenia.

We must—as I discussed in part in the previous chapter—take care of home in order to have anything of value to offer anyone else. By "home" I am referring to any number of actualities, including the condition of our own soul, our family, and the physical space in which we live, our place of business and the care of our teammates and employees, and the community or nation in which we live. Before we can move to *philoxenia* we must take care of *philadelphia*.

> Before we can love our neighbor, we must love and care for ourselves so we can have something to offer our neighbor.

As theologian and ethicist Elizabeth Newman wisely wrote, "Hospitality without a home (a place) is an oxymoron" and, paraphrasing Gordon Cosby, "hospitality flows out of identity and . . . if you do not know who you are, you cannot offer hospitality." Scripture calls us to offer a radical welcome to strangers, but we are not able to give what we do not have. Before we can love our neighbor, we must love and care for ourselves so we can have something to offer our neighbor. We must be hospitable to brother, sister, wife, husband, children, parents—and brothers and sisters in Christ. "So reach out and welcome one another." . . . "Offer hospitality to one another without grumbling." . . . "Love your spiritual family." Hospitality begins in *philadelphia*.

Then it gets better. I believe with all my heart that our lives are exponentially expanded, that we get bigger and everything we care about gets better when we move to *philoxenia*. We must be hospitable to strangers. This move is not optional for people of the Christian faith, so we must assume there is something beyond wonderful in this straightforward admonition to "entertain strangers" or to "show love unto strangers" or "keep an open house." Now that we are home, we are commanded to share home with strangers. To be hospitable leaders, we must embrace every part of what it means to move to *philoxenia*. *Philoxenia* is the opposite of *xenophobia*. *Xenophobia* is an irrational fear of people who are not like us. It is the antithesis of what the Scriptures teach us in both Old and New Testament. Hospitality—literally loving strangers—was a requirement for leaders in the early Christian church. A church leader must be "hospitable" or "enjoy having guests in his home." He or she must be a "lover of hospitality" or a "lover of loving strangers."

The great Henri Nouwen in his seminal work on Christian hospitality wrote about the necessary privilege of creating space for strangers that "it is possible for men and women and obligatory for Christians to offer an open and hospitable space where strangers can cast off their strangeness and become our fellow human beings." I find such hope and possibility in his words! He goes on, "If there is any concept worth restoring to its original depth and evocative potential, it is the concept of hospitality. . . . Old and New Testament stories not only show how serious our obligation is to welcome the stranger in our home, but they also tell us that guests are carrying precious gifts with them, which they are eager to reveal to a receptive host."

The mandate in Scripture to love the stranger is rooted in the fact that all of us who have been welcomed by God know what it is to have been strange to Him and His promises. Moses stressed this to the children of Israel after their deliverance from Egypt. "The stranger who dwells among you shall be to you as one born among you, and you shall love him as yourself; for you were strangers in the land of Egypt." The apostle Paul celebrated the deliverance from darkness of all who believe in Jesus and have been welcomed into covenant with God: "at that time you were without Christ, being aliens from the commonwealth of Israel and strangers from the covenants of promise, having no hope and without God in the world. But now in Christ Jesus you who once were far off have been brought near by the blood of Christ. . . . Now, therefore, you are no longer strangers and foreigners, but fellow citizens with the saints and members of the household of God. "

Each of us was once alienated from God. But thankfully, He loves the stranger. The fact that we have been welcomed home should move us to welcome as well. How can those of us who have received grace not be gracious? I hope to be among those who are welcomed to life everlasting by Jesus with these words: "I was a stranger and you invited me in," because I shared His heart to welcome people who are not like me.

The practice of hospitality is a central theme in the manners and customs of biblical times. Though the exact manner in which strangers were entertained was in flux over the several thousand years of history covered in Scripture, it is patently clear that God expected His people to organize their lives in a way that would always make room for them to be hospitable to guests. Strangers were to be greeted, fed, invited to stay—usually for several days—and entertained in a variety of ways. Ralph Gower wrote that "during and after the courses of the meal entertainment was provided in which readings of poetry and prose were given and in which there was music and dancing . . . and occasionally a display as in a cabaret act was performed."

I especially like this picture Gower paints: "It was possible for local people to look in on what was happening . . . the occasions were brilliantly lit so they could be seen from the darkness outside." This is a beautiful metaphor for believers who have been called out of darkness into marvelous light. This describes the hospitality of God. He invites strangers to come in out of the darkness and experience His light and life. Hospitable leaders share this state of mind. We are always inviting strangers in. This is our basic way of life. Henri Nouwen gets at this so well: "The term hospitality therefore, should not be limited to its literal sense of receiving a stranger in our house—though it is important never to forget or neglect that!—but as a fundamental attitude toward our fellow human being, which can be expressed in a great variety of ways." We must organize our lives and homes and organizations to constantly offer invitation to those outside of our circle of light. Everything about us should shout to the stranger, "Come in! Please, come in!"

And some of us have learned that when we entertain strangers we often entertain angels unaware. *Angel* means messenger. A good angel is a messenger from God. An angel of light.

So important was what one writer called "the law of hospitality" that the Jewish people believed God would send angels to test its practice. It is possible that a stranger might be an angel in disguise. Literally. Stranger things have happened. As a monk called Brother Jeremiah said, "We always treat guests as angels—just in case."

But, in a more earthy way, what I have experienced is that when I have opened my heart to people who are different from me, strange to me, they often are—or become—messengers from God. God uses them to impact my life and leadership in powerful ways. We must see the angel in every stranger. This is at the core of how a hospitable leader must view life.

There are many ways we could get at what it means to love strangers and what it looks like for strangers to become messengers from God. For me, probably the most significant way I have lived this out is through leading a congregation that is diverse in every imaginable way—including racially. There is not a dominant racial group in the leadership of the congregation I serve. That seems unbelievable even as I write it. But it is true nonetheless.

I am not the likely candidate to lead such an amazing diversity of people. I wish I could say I planned for this, but that would not be true. I grew up in Indiana with people pretty much like me: white, middle-class, suburban, Christian. Good people. Very little was ever said about race, and frankly, I just didn't give the subject much thought. The best one could say is that I was oblivious to the experiences of minorities in the United States. It would probably be a kindness to describe me as growing up simply indifferent to people who are not like me.

What happened? How did I end up leading as diverse a church as you can find in the world? Somehow in my life and leadership journey, something happened in my heart and I experienced a driving desire to know and love people who are not like me. And I found myself surrounded by people who felt the same way. I have championed this aspirational idea of hospitable leadership for years now, including this emphasis on learning to love people who are "strange" to us. But I am not sure which came first. Did I develop this thought to describe what had happened in my heart and experience, or did this value create the environment that caused it to happen? I have lived it for so long I don't even know. I do know, however, that a leader can create an environment of hospitality that causes people to love loving people who are not like them. And this is a glorious thing.

There are a multitude of things I do not understand about race. What I do understand is that I can only learn if I sit at the table with people who are not like me. People who come from different backgrounds and experiences and who often have a different perspective than I do. I have learned to be hospitable to strangers. I have learned to receive the hospitality of those who think I am strange. And I have learned that often, strangers become messengers from God who profoundly impact my life and help me lead in ways that I could never have led otherwise.

A profound experience for me was when I watched the verdict of the O.J. Simpson trial with my longtime associate pastor, Andrew McCleese. Like most Americans, I found myself sucked into the drama of the trial of the century and followed every twist and turn with great attention. Finally, the news came that the jury had returned a verdict. Andrew and I were at the office, so we jumped into the car and raced to my house to witness what the jury had decided. (We couldn't afford a television in our offices in those days.)

And then the verdict was announced. When O.J. was declared not guilty, I was apoplectic. I jumped up and yelled at the TV. I couldn't believe it! Then I noticed Andrew was still on the couch, and not only was he not angry, he seemed to be somewhat pleased. I was stunned. "Are you not upset?" I asked him. "Do you think that he is innocent?" I didn't wait for an answer. "He obviously is guilty! He should be punished for committing these heinous crimes!" Andrew just sat there.

> [We] can only learn if [we] sit at the table with people who are not like [us].

And then it hit me. I assumed that Andrew would feel the same way I felt about this. Or the same way that pretty much every white person in America felt. But . . . Andrew is not a white person. Did I mention that? Andrew is African-American. I had never even asked him what he thought. Thankfully, I had enough sense to turn off the TV, sit down, and ask him, "What am I missing here?" I respected Andrew greatly. But I had not made space for him to say anything.

Finally, he answered me. He told me that for him, the issue at that moment wasn't primarily about O.J.'s guilt or innocence. It was about the experience of a black man in America. It was about supposed evidence that had been collected by a police officer who had offered racial epithets in his past. Andrew said, "Do you know I still drive through certain towns, frightened to be pulled over by a cop? Do you understand that just a few years ago it wasn't all that uncommon for someone who looks like me to be hung from a tree without the benefit of a jury at all? Do you know what it is like to be a black man in America?" For once in my life I was utterly speechless. No. I didn't know. I just assumed that everyone would think and feel just like me. I had no idea. Worse . . . I didn't know that I didn't know.

In that moment, Andrew was hospitable to me in my lack of knowing. Or what some may inhospitably call my ignorance. Look, I still think O.J. was guilty. And for the record, I believe that the vast majority of those who serve our communities in law enforcement do the right thing the vast majority of the time. But the point is that Andrew and I were strangers in our experiences of race. We could have sat on opposite sides of the room yelling at one another. That's what many in our society seem to do. Instead, we chose to sit and talk and listen, and to love one another in our strangeness. And on that day and on many others, Andrew became to me a messenger from God.

After all of that, you may be surprised that I seldom talk about race. But I care deeply about the divisions in our culture around this issue. What would happen if we would simply be hospitable to one another? If we would love people—not tolerate, but love people—who are different from us in this and other ways? What would happen if we looked at every stranger and assumed they were a messenger from God?

God has spoken to me time and time again through people who are not like me in any number of ways. Like the beautiful woman who contracted AIDS through a dirty needle she used to sustain her heroin addiction. I would visit her in the hospital as she was dying, and she would whisper words of encouragement. She taught me how to suffer graciously. Or like the wife of a multimillionaire Wall Street analyst who practiced a rare servant leadership and taught me how to leverage privilege to serve others. Or like the Jewish community leader who taught me how to shake things up to care for the poor. Or the former Black Panther—who sat through three of my Welcome to the

Church teaching rotations because he couldn't believe that a white guy like me would really love and accept him. He taught me how to risk trusting people I might have reason to be suspicious of. Or like the first-generation immigrant who taught me how to prepare for my children's future. I watched him start with nothing and go on to earn a doctorate while raising his two children to be a medical doctor and a lawyer. Or like the sanitation worker who was orphaned and grew up on the mean streets of Patterson, New Jersey. He taught me how to love my kids with the passion of someone who had never known a dad or mom. Or the Catholic man whose world was rocked by Jesus late in his life and who loved our church so much he would sit in his car on our undeveloped church property and pray at five o'clock every morning. He taught me how to approach God with simple faith and expectation and to love our church enough to sacrifice for it every day.

In some way each of these people was strange to me. And I to them. But when we love loving strangers, it opens new worlds of possibility. Strangers become messengers from God.

I can't help but think about that story in Genesis when Abraham "looked up and saw three men standing nearby. When he saw them, he hurried from the entrance of his tent to meet them and bowed low to the ground. . . . So Abraham hurried into the tent to Sarah. 'Quick,' he said, 'get three seahs of the finest flour and knead it and bake some bread.' Then he ran to the herd and selected a choice, tender calf and gave it to a servant, who hurried to prepare it."

At some point in the story, Abraham realized that one of these men was a messenger from God. Or God himself. "Then the Lord said, 'I will certainly return to you about this time a year from now. At that time your wife Sarah will have a son.'" This message from God changed Abraham's destiny and the destiny of the world. But Abraham would not have received the message if not for his hospitality. Note the response when Abraham saw these three strangers; it was *hurried, hurried, quick, ran,* and *hurried.*

I think that's what leaders should do whenever we encounter someone who seems strange to us. We should *hurry, hurry, quick, run,* and *hurry* to welcome that stranger. To invite them in. To prepare a feast for them. To entertain them. To know them better. Who knows? That stranger may be a messenger from God who will change our world forever.

Leadership Take-Homes

1. **Make the move from Philadelphia to Philoxenia.** While it's relatively easy to care for those we know and like, we are called to love complete strangers, people different from us in any number of ways.

2. **Welcoming the stranger isn't a nicety—it's a necessity.** To lead a diversity of people with diverse gifts, we must practice the scriptural mandate of welcoming the person who is strange to us.

3. **Hospitality requires a spirit of understanding.** To practice hospitable leadership, we must acknowledge that others have experiences and points of view different from our own.

Sources

"Remember to welcome strangers": Hebrews 13:2 NCV.
"Do not forget to show hospitality": Hebrews 13:2.
"men are from Mars": John Gray, *Men Are from Mars, Women Are from Venus* (New York: Harper Collins, 1993).

"Keep on loving each other": Hebrews 13:1–2 NCV.

Philadelphia: Hebrews 13:1. biblestudytools.com/lexicons/greek/nas/phila delphia.htmlhttps://www.biblestudytools.com/lexicons/greek/kjv/philox enia.html

Philoxenia: Hebrews 13:2. https://www.biblestudytools.com/lexicons/greek /kjv/philoxenia.html

"Hospitality without a home": Elizabeth Newman, *Untamed Hospitality: Welcoming God and Other Strangers* (Grand Rapids: Brazos Press, 2007), 53, 186.

"So reach out and welcome one another.": Romans 15:7 MESSAGE.

"Offer hospitality to one another": 1 Peter 4:9.

"Love your spiritual family.": 1 Peter 2:17 MESSAGE.

"entertain strangers": Hebrews 13:2 NKJV.

"show love unto strangers": Hebrews 13:2 ASV.

"keep an open house": Matthew 5:16 MESSAGE.

"hospitable": 1 Timothy 3:2.

"enjoy having guests": 1 Timothy 3:2 TLB.

"lover of hospitality": Titus 1:8 KJV.

"it is possible for men and women": Henri Nouwen, *Reaching Out: The Three Movements of the Spiritual Life* (New York: Doubleday, 1986), 86.

"The stranger who dwells among you": Leviticus 19:34 NKJV.

"at that time you were without Christ": Ephesians 2:12–13, 19 NKJV.

"I was a stranger": Matthew 25:35–40.

"during and after the courses": Ralph Gower, *The New Manners and Customs of Bible Times* (Chicago: Moody Press, 1987), 248–249.

"The term hospitality therefore": Nouwen, *Reaching Out*, 67.

"the law of hospitality": Christine Pohl, *Making Room: Recovering Hospitality as a Christian Tradition* (Grand Rapids: Eerdmans Publishing, 1999), 85.

"We always treat guests": Brother Jeremiah as quoted by Alan W. Jones in *Soul Making: The Desert Way of Spirituality* (San Francisco: HarperSanFrancisco, 1985), 13.

"looked up and saw three men": Genesis 18:2.

"Quick": Genesis 18:6–7.

"Then the Lord said": Genesis 18:10 NCV.

4

Radical Hospitality Produces Revolutionary Results

Asbury Seminary Professor Christine Pohl wrote that "Christian hospitality has always had a subversive countercultural dimension. 'Hospitality is resistance.'" I agree. Hospitable leadership, if properly understood and practiced, has a radical edge. By its very nature hospitality holds the potential to bring revolutionary change—to overturn the way things are but shouldn't be. Hospitality must not be equated with people sitting around singing "Kum ba yah." Leaders must move things forward. We must lead ourselves and others to get things done, solve problems, and actualize possibilities. We must not be satisfied with the present state or conditions. Our world needs revolutionary change.

On a grand scale, things seem to just not be working. The very environment around us feels charged with an almost tangible negativity. *Polarization* is a word I am weary of hearing, but it is an apt description of the atmosphere invading our politics and our discussions around class, gender, race, religion, and more. I believe that this divisiveness in the climate of the world at large affects most things our lives are about. I frequently deal with families roiled by divisions in national politics. I talk to businesspeople who strain to succeed against the gravitational pull of local, state, and national governments so divided it seems that little of help ever gets done. I hear from teachers who are discouraged from simply teaching kids because their schools are ruptured by strife. And I have personal experience with how a general hostility in the atmosphere around us threatens the unity of churches and distracts far too many Christ-followers from focusing on what life with God and one another should really be about.

Our world needs a climate change. I want to be part of a movement of leaders who commit to a radical hospitality and together lead a revolution of positive change. Hospitality is resistance.

Regardless of your thoughts about Christianity, if you are a leader, you should want to study the leadership practices of Jesus and His earliest followers. Why? They inarguably led the most powerful—and when authentically practiced, positive—change effort in the history of the world. If you want to learn about leadership that brings results, look at Jesus. And the framework in which His leadership was practiced was—again—hospitality.

The seed of the revolution Jesus launched is unearthed when we see who He sat at the table with. New Testament scholar Scott Bartchy writes, "It would be difficult to overestimate the importance of table fellowship for the cultures of the Mediterranean basin in the first century of our era. . . . Being welcomed at a table for the purpose of eating food with another person had become a ceremony richly symbolic of friendship, intimacy and unity." Jesus resisted the way things were in His world when He ate with tax collectors, who were considered traitors by their Jewish brothers, and with flagrant sinners. The leaders of the Jewish religion were scandalized. "But the Pharisees and the teachers of the law who belonged to their sect complained to his disciples, 'Why do you eat and drink with tax collectors and sinners?'" It is difficult to fully comprehend, or explain, how this simple act of hospitality modeled radical inclusivity. But it did. The hospitable leadership of Jesus slammed against the walls of division that stood between various kinds of people in that time and place.

We get a further hint of the revolutionary nature of hospitable leadership when Jesus was accused of being a "glutton and a drunkard." This language comes from the Mosaic law, which taught that a rebellious son was to be taken by his parents to the elders of the city. "They shall say to the elders, 'This son of ours is stubborn and rebellious. He will not obey us. He is a glutton and a drunkard.'" The punishment for a son's rebellion was death by stoning. The fact that Jesus was eating and drinking with sinners was so scandalous that the religious fathers of His day accused Him of being a rebellious son. Their judgment was that He should be summarily executed.

The fact is that Jesus often welcomed people who were completely other than He was. The only sinless man in history ate and drank with sinners. And His hospitality created the space where those completely other could become like Him. He didn't just hang out with sinners. That would not be leadership. He influenced the people He hung out with. He gave them the power to change. He challenged them to become leaders themselves. And when they did, they led a revolution that changed the world forever.

Jesus did not just welcome His moral opposites though. He also constantly included those who had been excluded before. He did this because it was right. But while doing what was right, He also leveraged His influence by dramatically expanding the number of people who could join Him in His cause. The best example of this might be His inclusion of women in a way that was unheard of in His day. As Dietrich Bonhoeffer wrote, "Jesus gave women human dignity. . . . Prior to Jesus, women were regarded as inferior human beings, religiously speaking."

Jesus not only welcomed women, He also invited them to join His leadership team. Obviously, the twelve apostles were men. But women played a role in Jesus' ministry never seen until His time. I like the way N. T. Wright observes that when the male disciples "all forsake Jesus and run away . . . it is the women who come first to the tomb, who are the first to see the risen Jesus, and are the first to be entrusted with the news that he has been raised from the dead. This is of incalculable significance. Mary Magdalene and the others are the apostles to the apostles."

When Jesus included women, He more than doubled His influence. All of a sudden He had a leadership relationship with an entire population that previously had been sidelined. Part of the revolutionary aspect of hospitable leadership is that we invite people to join our team and help us to fulfill our mission who may have never even sat at the table before.

In Luke's gospel we see an example of how Jesus employs uncompromising radical inclusiveness to multiply His leadership influence. "A woman named Martha opened her home to him. She had a sister called Mary, who sat at the Lord's feet listening to what he said. But Martha was distracted by all the preparations that had to be made. She came to him and asked, 'Lord, don't you care that my sister has left me to do the work by myself? Tell her to help me!'" In this well-known story, Martha played the role of host, while Mary sat in the room normally reserved for men. When we read that she "sat at the Lord's feet listening to what he said," our eyes should open wide to what this phrase indicates. It signals that Mary had adopted the posture of a leader in training. She was learning in the manner a student would learn, "at the feet of" a rabbi, in order to become a rabbi himself. Or now, herself. This was great for Mary. It was also great for Jesus and His cause.

The inclusion of women at this level of potential leadership meant that Jesus had twice the number of potential disciples and leaders to recruit from. It sounds dumb to say this, but He was so smart. John Ortberg writes that "this radical value of women meant that they began to take on unusually prominent roles of leadership in the early church. Roughly half of the households Paul mentions that form the infrastructure for the early church are headed by women."

I am so grateful to have been surrounded by a multitude of strong male leaders in my leadership journey. The Christian church desperately needs strong male leadership. But I cannot imagine what I would have missed—what the world around me would have missed—if we didn't have powerfully gifted women leading at every leadership level in our church.

I don't really mean to make this about women though. The larger point is that hospitable leaders are intentional about welcoming people who may not have been invited before. It astounds me when I see leaders who only speak to their "base."

> **Hospitable leaders are intentional about welcoming people who may not have been invited before.**

This may be a way to protect what they have or to maintain power, but it is not how to expand power or to multiply influence for good.

The leaders of the early Christian church continued the revolutionary hospitality of Jesus. And they multiplied their influence for good all over the world. The apostle Paul in particular continued leading with this insurgent edge. He fought vociferously for the right of the previously excluded Gentiles to sit at the table—literally—with the other early church leaders, all of whom were Jewish. And as a result, the church expanded dramatically.

In a further show of radical resistance against the accepted order of things, Paul not only condemned slave traders but welcomed slaves to his table. His relationship with the runaway slave Onesimus brought breathtaking implications. Paul called him his son. He said that Onesimus was part of his team. And Paul wrote to Onesimus's master, Philemon, that he should be welcomed back in the same way Paul had been welcomed by Philemon. This was good for Onesimus, of course, but from a leadership perspective it was also good for the cause. An entire population of God's children—previously sidelined—were welcomed to Christ and His mission. Hospitable. Leadership.

Paul wanted everybody to be welcomed. He laid the groundwork for progress still advancing today when he wrote this to the Galatians: "There is neither Jew nor Gentile, neither slave nor free, nor is there male and female, for you are all one in Christ Jesus." In Jewish culture, where only a firstborn male received the inheritance of the father, Paul taught that everybody—women, slaves, Gentiles, second-born sons, third-born sons, adopted daughters and sons, anybody, everybody—had the right of the firstborn son. One may argue the finer points of Paul's teachings regarding some of these issues of inclusion, but it is undeniable that he carried forward the heart of Jesus to bring a revolution of welcome. And, in no small part because of his hospitable leadership, that revolution has expanded for two thousand years.

Who should be invited to what we are doing? For me the answer is everyone. Everyone is invited. Please don't misunderstand me. I am inviting people I want to influence. I am inviting people I want to join my team. I want to create an environment of welcome where truth can be spoken and lives can be changed.

This begins, however, with radical inclusion. I cannot influence people who are not there.

The polarization of our society is damaging to any effort to achieve anything great. If we do not learn how to sit at the table with one another, we will never accomplish much together. Empty seats are opportunities missed. Sadly, it seems that more and more people just want to be with people who are like them: who look like them, think like them, and want the same things they do. If we lead with this perspective, then we are terribly limited. Leadership by exclusion is leadership by subtraction.

The polarization of our society is damaging to any effort to achieve anything great.

The political climate in the United States offers a painful example of the limiting nature of division and inversion. Some businesses in the area where I live and work plainly state that if you voted for who they consider to be the "wrong person," you are not welcome. Limiting. I know folks who will only attend church with people who have the same political views they do and who presumably vote as they do. Limiting. We all have probably witnessed friendships—and families!—torn apart by political disagreement. Tragic.

Christian leaders must revolt against this societal craziness. Sadly though, too often I see even Christian leaders who let it be known that if you are not in sync with their views on issues, policies, and politics, you are not welcome at their table. Inhospitable. Leaders?

At the risk of sounding inhospitable myself, from where I sit, leadership by exclusion is immoral. It is also unwise. Even if my goal is only to persuade others to my views, I cannot persuade people I do not welcome.

A recent presidential election provided an interesting leadership challenge for me. It affected the environment of our nation in a way most of us had never experienced. It's as if every polarizing issue surfaced and every seed of division produced its unpalatable fruit. I'm not blaming either candidate. I sense that regardless of who had prevailed, we would be in a similar state of unpleasantness, just with a different segment of our population in a state of perpetual outrage.

As I have mentioned, the congregation I serve is incredibly diverse. There is no dominant people group. It's wonderful! And it's challenging. I suspect that somewhere near half of us voted for the Republican and the other half of us voted for the Democrat. Please don't judge. I was reminded during this season that the church I lead is not inoculated from the overall climate of the world around us. The very air seemed heavy with potential division. I'm guessing that unless you live or lead in a place where almost everybody is like you, you felt this too. An inhospitable—ugly—environment.

A longtime leader in our congregation, an African-American criminal defense attorney, urgently wanted to talk with me. "I know you don't ever speak about partisan politics. I don't know how you voted," he said, "but I trust you and I believe you need to speak to our congregation about this election." He was deeply concerned that the inflammation in our society at large would infect our church. He went on to explain to me—a very white male, in case you haven't seen my picture—why so many African-Americans felt so aggrieved by this particular election. He shared some of his personal experiences with racial injustice. I was moved. I shared my thoughts and feelings from my background and experiences as well. He was grateful.

And then, on the Sunday after the most divisive of national elections, when much of our nation seemingly was yelling at each other, I gave a very carefully crafted talk to one of the most diverse congregations in the land. After which there seemed to be a corporate sigh of relief. People from both sides were magnanimous and generously thanked me. What did I speak about? Hospitality. Why? Because hospitality is resistance to the accepted order of things. Hospitality says we will not stand for division. We will not shout at each other. We will not look at one another and suspect dark motives. We will not judge each other. We will celebrate the opportunity to do life with people who are totally different than we are—even strange to us. We will listen to them. We will speak our truth to them. We will welcome them.

I knew that if I could get everyone back to the table, I could lead them. You can't lead people if they aren't at the table.

Dr. Martin Luther King Jr. was a hospitable leader in so many ways. He was a results-oriented revolutionary. Get this: He *protested* in a way that invited people in. He was merciful to the ignorant. He didn't just say, "I have a dream." He did so much more. He created an environment in which his dreams and the dreams of countless others could come to life. He got results.

One of the most wonderful autobiographies I have ever read is technically not an autobiography—it is a collection of Dr. King's own words edited by Clayborne Carson, *The Autobiography of Martin Luther King Jr.* As I read this years ago, I was struck by King's insistence on peaceful protest. One of his great difficulties was his struggle against those in the civil rights movement who wanted to take a more confrontational—or even violent—approach to advance their righteous cause. Dr. King was a coalition builder. He brought people to the table. He saw the best in others even when he had every reason not to.

I was moved by the compassion he displayed toward people who did not understand his cause. In the election of 1960 he gave both Republican Richard Nixon and Democrat John F. Kennedy the opportunity to win his tacit support—though his organization was officially nonpartisan. He discussed at some length how, when he first met Kennedy, the future president did not have a grasp or comprehension of the struggle for civil rights. "He knew that segregation was morally wrong and he certainly intellectually committed himself to integration, but I could see that he didn't have the emotional involvement then. He had not really been involved enough in and with the problem. He didn't know too many Negroes personally. He had never really had the personal experience of knowing the deep groans and passionate yearnings of the Negro for freedom, because he just didn't know Negroes generally and he hadn't had any experience in the civil rights struggle."

Dr. King then shared that after JFK won the nomination, they had another conversation: "I talked with him over at his house in Georgetown, and in that short period he had really learned a great deal about civil rights. . . ." Finally, after President Kennedy's assassination, Dr. King offered, "His last speech on race relations was the most earnest, human, and profound appeal for understanding and justice that any President has uttered since the first days of the republic."

Why was I so moved by this? Martin Luther King Jr. created an environment of welcome where a future president, who simply didn't understand the struggle for civil rights, could change and grow. The result of this was evidenced when the Civil Rights Act of 1964 was passed. President Kennedy's successor, Lyndon B. Johnson, stood against many of his fellow Democrats to join arms with Republicans to legislate changes in civil rights that changed our country forever. Yes, there is still much work to do, but Dr. King's dream still lives.

Jesus said, "Settle matters quickly with your adversary who is taking you to court. Do it while you are still together on the way, or your adversary may hand you over to the judge, and the judge may hand you over to the officer, and you may be thrown into prison." It's interesting that He assumed adversaries would be together on the way to court. He assumed that they would have the opportunity to talk about how to reconcile their differences before judgment was rendered. Tragically, we often render judgment before any meaningful discussions are had. Therefore, when someone doesn't agree about public policy, they issue judgment: "You are a racist," "You don't love our nation," "You don't care about the poor," "You hate immigrants," or "You don't care about the victims of crime." When we judge each other this way we are all sentenced to a prison of sorts. And we miss out on the power of a unified focus on what we can do together to bring positive change.

I highly value my relationship with Richard Trenk, the longtime township attorney of West Orange. He and his wife, Nancy, a Superior Court judge, have been friends of mine and Sharon for years. From the outside someone might think we have little in common. He is Jewish. I am a Christian. I am a pastor. He is a lawyer. I could go on. º the years we have had numerous conversations about issues of great importance in our country, county, and township, often while we watched his son Robert and my son Christian play traveling soccer and baseball together. Frankly, most of the time we have disagreed on matters of politics and specific policies. However, there is so much we have in common. Like me, Richard passionately loves his family. And our community. And he cares deeply about issues of poverty and injustice. Over the years he has led key initiatives in our township to help the poor and care for the less fortunate in a variety of ways. Most recently he successfully led an effort for West

> **When we judge each other . . . we miss out on the power of a unified focus on what we can do together to bring positive change.**

Orange to become the first municipality in New Jersey to launch Operation HOPE (the Heroin-Opiate Prevention Effort).

To my great joy, when Richard gets all wrapped up in a cause like this, he usually calls me. "Would you mind getting your church involved in this? Could you come and speak to the Town Council in favor of this program? Would you appear with me on television to discuss this issue?" I remember only one occasion when I said no. He wanted me to get involved in an issue that was not in alignment with what I believe Scripture teaches about a certain social issue. We spoke honestly. He did not judge me. I did not judge him. And the next time he wanted my help, thankfully, he reached out again. And I jumped in.

I might add that over the years this Jewish attorney has helped this Christian pastor lead a Christian church to succeed in a township that is 30 percent Jewish. He has always represented the interests of the township first, as is his duty. But whenever possible he has partnered with us to help us be a force for good—and I would say God—in our town.

I am encouraged, and surprised, when I read about towering leaders of the past who carefully cultivated relationships with their political opposites. The tradition is longstanding: Franklin Delano Roosevelt famously regaled friend and foe in the White House on most evenings. He personally mixed and served the drinks. Republican President Dwight Eisenhower was roundly criticized by members of his own party because he especially enjoyed hosting two Democrats: Speaker of the House Sam Rayburn and Senate Majority Leader Lyndon B. Johnson. Republican President Ronald Reagan loved spending time with his ferocious political adversary, Speaker of the House Tip O'Neill. They swapped stories and laughed heartily at each other's jokes.

These leaders developed mutual respect. They talked about their disagreements. They debated—heatedly at times—but in the spirit of hospitality. They worked to find common ground whenever possible. They solved problems. And they led. Not perfectly . . . but one has the sense they got important things done. That tends to happen when a leader welcomes people in.

I watch some of what passes for debate in our nation today and I sometimes think, *I wish you would take each other out to dinner.* I read articles in which one Christian leader criticizes another for this or that reason and I think, *I wish you guys would spend more time together.* More than likely you can look around your company and see a couple of people, or maybe teams or departments, in a communications cold war, and you might think, *I wish they would do lunch together more often.* We could get so much more done if we would be hospitable to one another in spite of our differences.

I say we can make it happen. We can insist on creating hospitable environments that unleash the potential inherent when people from all kinds of backgrounds work together to accomplish something great.

Millions of people have been captivated by a simple piece of art created by a graffiti master—painter—artist—activist—filmmaker, named Banksy. It is a painting of a protester throwing a Molotov cocktail, which morphs into a bouquet of beautiful flowers in his hand. Some refer to this image as "rage," others as "flower thrower." Banksy, who has somehow managed to keep his identity secret, did not name it. But "outraged flower thrower" seems to capture it well.

It seems like everyone is outraged—outraged!—by any number of things going on in our world today. And we probably should be. The question that interests me most is how can I lead effectively in this environment? How can I best affect positive change? Henri Nouwen said that we need to move from hostility to hospitality. I think this is the best approach to tackle problems small and large and to expand our influence for good in ever-widening circles.

In the big picture, the status quo is not working. Molotov cocktails are hurled in 140-character tweets and memes, and talk-show debates, and late-night not-really-all-that-funny jokes. We need a culture of flower throwers. There is plenty to protest, but let's lead a new kind of revolution. Let's create environments of welcome where God and good things can happen.

Leadership Take-Homes

1. **Hospitality is resistance.** Hospitable leadership has a radical edge with the potential to produce revolutionary results. Jesus was a radically hospitable leader whose message and methods changed history.

2. **Inclusion multiplies influence.** We cannot lead or influence people who are not at our table.

3. **Hospitable leaders create time and space to learn what they do not know.** We must learn about one another, and about our experiences, our problems, our ideas.

Sources

"Christian hospitality has always": Christine Pohl, *Making Room: Recovering Hospitality as a Christian Tradition* (Grand Rapids: Eerdmans Publishing, 1999), 61.

"It would be difficult to overestimate": S. Scott Bartchy, "Table Fellowship" in *Dictionary of Jesus and the Gospels* (Downers Grove: InterVarsity Press, 1992), 796.

"But the Pharisees and the teachers": Luke 5:30.

"glutton and a drunkard": Luke 7:34.

"They shall say to the elders": Deuteronomy 21:20.

"Jesus gave women human dignity": Dietrich Bonhoeffer, as quoted by John Ortberg in *Who Is This Man?* (Grand Rapids: Zondervan, 2012), 51.

"all forsake Jesus and run away": N. T. Wright, "Women's Service in the Church," NTWrightPage, ntwrightpage.com/2016/07/12/womens -service-in-the-church-the-biblical-basis.

"She had a sister called Mary": Luke 10:38–40.

"this radical value of women meant": John Ortberg, *Who Is this Man*, 55.

Philemon: Philemon 1–25.

"There is neither Jew nor Gentile": Galatians 3:28.

"He knew that segregation was morally wrong": Clayborne Carson, *The Autobiography of Martin Luther King Jr.* (New York: Warner Books, 1998), 320, 143, 144, 236.

"Settle matters quickly with your adversary": Matthew 5:25.

We need to move from hostility to hospitality: Henri Nouwen, *Reaching Out* (New York: Doubleday, 1986), 67.

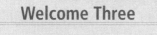

Welcome Three

DREAMS

5

Head Full of Dreams

Trappist monk Thomas Merton, in his classic spiritual autobiography *The Seven Storey Mountain*, wrote about an encounter with the headmistress of an English boarding school he attended as a young boy: Mrs. Pearce "was a balky and rather belligerent-looking woman" who was dismissive of Thomas's father because he was an artist. She asked Thomas's aunt, in his presence: "'Does he want to be a dilettante like his father?' said Mrs. Pearce roughly, surveying me with a rather outraged expression." His aunt replied kindly to the severe headmistress that Thomas wanted to be a journalist. She and Thomas had just been discussing the possibility as a path to his ultimate dream of being a novelist. "'Nonsense,' said Mrs. Pearce . . . 'He might as well get some sensible ideas into his head . . . and not go out into the world with his head full of dreams.' . . . 'Boy! Don't become a dilettante, do you hear?'"

As I read Merton's words, I pictured this scene in my mind and could feel the angst of a young boy shamed, simply because he had a dream. I rather prefer the sound of Coldplay ringing in my ears: ". . . you can see the change you wanted . . . with a head full, a head full of dreams." I like what I feel when I hear that song played and those words sung.

Leaders have inordinate power to create environments where dreamers and their dreams can flourish. Conversely, leaders also often have the terrible power to engender environments where dreamers are discouraged and their dreams are crushed. In extreme cases, dream-killing environments may be spawned by a leader whose heart is dark and who out of that darkness speaks harsh and destructive words or worse. More often, I think dream-negative environments exist because even well-intentioned leaders too often do not pay careful attention to the dreams of those they lead.

Leaders usually have dreams of our own, or ones for the organization we lead, but that does not mean that we intentionally welcome dreamers or entertain their dreams. If we are not careful, we may practice a benign neglect when we should be proactive dream provocateurs. Leaders should use whatever power we have to celebrate dreamers and challenge them to dream ever bigger. We should inspire people to refine their dreams and to believe and pray and work and sacrifice to make those dreams come true. Simply put: Hospitable leaders are hospitable to people and to their dreams. We love it when we find ourselves leading people whose heads—and hearts—are full of dreams.

Jesus articulated a leadership that is hospitable to dreams when He promised "life in all its fullness," or as *The Message* has it, "more and better life than they ever dreamed of." This promise in John 10:10 is a central theme of my life and leadership. How does someone live "more and better life than they ever dreamed of"? By living the life God dreams for them. I introduced this concept in my last book, *Live 10*, and over the past few years my understanding of what Jesus was saying in this verse, and the context in which He said it, has expanded considerably. I am fascinated with the seldom discussed yet profound leadership implications of this well-known passage. Let me unpack this for a moment; I think you will find the detail is worth it.

When Jesus made this "more and better life than they ever dreamed of" promise, He was in the midst of contrasting two fundamentally different types of leadership: dream-killing leadership and dream-hospitable leadership. Or more specific to His terminology, bad leaders (or shepherds), who steal life from their followers, and good leaders (or shepherds), who give more and better life to those they lead than they had even dreamed of.

John's gospel tells us that "Jesus was in Jerusalem at the time of Hanukkah, the Festival of Dedication." Hanukkah is a feast that celebrates the victory of the Jewish Maccabeans in their uprising against Greek oppression in 165 BC, as well as the miracle that occurred when a supernatural flow of oil fueled the candles in the temple during its rededication. Important to this leadership discussion is the fact that Hanukkah is also a time when the Jewish people reflect on the failures of their leaders during the years preceding the Maccabean uprising. This failed leadership had nearly caused the Jews to lose their very identity as a people and to become disconnected from God and their destiny. The leaders of Judaism had compromised with a succession of Greek rulers, which led to a Hellenization that threatened the very essence of Judaism. These failed leaders—or bad shepherds—sold out in order to provide for their own safety, to line their pockets, and to garner position and privilege. They did it at the expense of the people they were responsible to lead and in defiance of God and His plans for His people.

In his commentary on the gospel of John, Gary M. Burge writes that "Hanukkah thus became a season that asked hard questions about failed leadership and false shepherds. . . . During the week when Jesus gave his good shepherd sermon, synagogues were reading prophetic critiques of leadership."

Here, for example, is Ezekiel's scathing prophetic critique of the wrong kind of leadership: leaders who only take care of themselves and do not care for the needs of those they lead. "Woe to the shepherds of Israel who only take care of themselves! Should not shepherds take care of the flock? . . . You have ruled them harshly and brutally. . . . As surely as I live, declares the Sovereign Lord, because my flock lacks a shepherd . . . and because my shepherds did not search for my flock but cared for themselves rather than for my flock . . . I am against the shepherds and will hold them accountable. . . ."

This reminds me of a term Dietrich Bonhoeffer used to refer to Adolf Hitler and leaders like him. He called these bad shepherds "*mis-leaders*." Bonhoeffer gave a speech just two days after Hitler's election that proved prophetic. He intimated that if a leader did not understand that his authority was derived from God, and did not use his position and power to serve the people, then "the image of the leader will pass over into the image of the mis-leader, and he will be acting in a criminal way not only towards those he leads, but also towards himself. . . . He has to lead the individual into his own maturity." Bonhoeffer proclaimed Hitler a mis-leader before his regime had even been fully formed. But one does not have to be a Hitler, or one of Ezekiel's blatantly evil shepherds, to be a "mis-leader." In my view, a mis-leader—or bad shepherd, or inhospitable leader—could be a headmistress who crushes the dreams of a young boy, or a pastor who makes everything about him, or a business leader who acts as if she thinks that everyone in her employ exists just to make her dreams come true.

In John 10 then, we are told how Jesus stood against the backdrop of failed shepherds and mis-leaders—in the context of Hanukkah—and described a new kind of leadership, declaring himself a new kind of leader. He said He is the Good Shepherd. "A thief is only there to steal and kill and destroy. I came so they can have real and eternal life, more and better life than they ever dreamed of. I am the Good Shepherd. The Good Shepherd puts the sheep before himself, sacrifices himself if necessary."

"Good shepherd" is a beautiful description of a hospitable leader. This is about more than not being a bad shepherd. This is about being a leader who, when people hear your voice, they want to follow you. They know that you will lead them to green pastures and quiet waters and soul-refreshing righteous possibilities. You do not rule people. You lead them. And you do not only care for their present needs, but are always promising more and better life than they ever dreamed of. You are a good shepherd. You are hospitable to people and their dreams.

History is littered with leaders who appeared to believe that the primary purpose of their leader power was to make their own dreams come true. Of course leaders must have dreams, and the bigger our dream, the better. But I submit that a central emphasis of our dream must be to serve the dreams of the people we lead. We must be able to focus on the goals of the entity we are leading—a company, a family, a football team, a nation—while focusing on the dreams of the individuals in it.

I have written at length in the past about how "moral leaders inspire, influence and empower others to self-actualization and the accomplishment of mission." That's pretty standard leadership jargon, unless you laser focus on the juxtaposition of "self-actualization" and "the accomplishment of mission." *Self-actualization* here refers, at least in part, to the dreams of those we lead. *Accomplishment of mission* refers to the dream of the thing we are leading.

My experience is that the default position of many leaders is to go all-in for the accomplishment of mission, far too often at the expense of the self-actualization of those who people the organization. If we are not careful, we will find ourselves in the ranks of those mis-leaders who have led people to achieve the leader's dream while ignoring, or at least not focusing on, the dreams—and perhaps not even the most basic needs—of those being led.

I frequently tell my congregation that I get up every day to do everything in my power to help them see their God-inspired dreams come true. It's amazing how people respond to a leader who they know is hospitable to their dreams. Steven Pressfield uses powerful leadership language in his historical novel about Alexander the Great. Alexander explained that what made his armies so wildly successful was the heart of the individual soldier and each soldier's will to fight. His soldiers' hearts were forged—and their wills inspired—in response to Alexander's passionate leadership. He poignantly describes how the first time he led men into battle, "I was so overcome I could not stay myself from weeping. . . . I was moved by the sight of them in such brilliant order, by their scars and their silence, the weathered creasing of their faces. When the men saw my state, they returned my devotion, for they knew I would burst my heart for them."

I love this picture. Alexander's men marched into victorious battle again and again with burning hearts in response to a leader they knew would "burst [his] heart" for them. As a leader I want people to hear my voice, and passionately and willingly follow me because they know I am not just leading them to fulfill *my* God-given dreams. My heart bursts for *them*. I want to lead *them* to more and better life than *they* ever dreamed of.

> If we are not careful, we will find ourselves in the ranks of those mis-leaders who have led people to achieve the leader's dream while ignoring, or at least not focusing on, the dreams . . . of those being led.

Richard Daft writes that there are five basic types of leadership power in organizations: *legitimate power* is derived from occupying a formal position of authority; *reward power* "stems from the authority to bestow rewards"; *coercive power* allows someone to "punish or recommend punishment"; *expert power* is the result of someone having more expertise than others; and *referent power* "comes from leader personality characteristics that command followers' identification, respect, and admiration."

I would like to suggest a sixth basic type of leader power. *Hospitable power.* Hospitable power is power willingly and passionately given to a leader by his or her followers because they know the leader is hospitable to them and their dreams. Because they know the leader's heart bursts for them. Because they know the leader is a good shepherd who will lead them to more and better life.

To be hospitable to people's dreams does not mean that we are focused only on their dreams, and it certainly does not mean that we are encouraging people to focus only on their dreams either. One of the greatest gifts we can give our followers is the opportunity to dream in an environment that is not just about them. Jesus promised more and better life than ever dreamed of in a much larger context than the dreams of any one person. He wanted us to see our dreams in light of His dreams for the world. We can lead people to a fully actualized life when we provoke them to dream the dreams God dreams for them in alignment with His dreams for the world.

We can extrapolate infinitely practical principles from this larger concept; dreamers need to feel connected to a great mission. They need to know that life is about more than just them. David Brooks wrote that "life is essentially a moral drama, not a hedonistic one." I would say that leaders best serve people when we engage them in a great moral cause.

Laszlo Bock "leads Google's people function which includes all areas related to the attraction, development and retention of 'Googlers.'" He makes the case that Google's mission "to organize the world's information and make it universally accessible and useful" is at its core a moral mission. He writes that "this kind of mission gives individuals' work meaning, because it is a moral rather than a business goal. The most powerful movements in history have had moral motivations. . . ." Bock believes that this broad moral mission provides the space "for Googlers and others to create wonderful things" and that "the most talented people on the planet want an aspiration that is also inspiring." I like that Bock argues for the practicality of a clearly articulated moral mission for an organization and connects the success of the individuals who people it back to that greater cause. Leaders must use power to engage people in the advance of good in this world. We must challenge people to dream big dreams that make sense in a larger moral framework.

Our mission statement at The Life Christian Church attempts to capture the synergistic possibilities of inspiring an individual's dreams in the larger context of an organizational mission to do good in the world at large: "To inspire people to the life God dreams for them as we spread his love in ever-widening circles." I want to inspire people to pursue their dreams with the larger moral mission firmly in mind.

I believe that whether they are aware of it or not, people want to be called to dream in light of the great moral drama. The fight between good and evil. Part of what great leaders do is invite people to an adventure that subsumes their potentially self-centered, small lives in a cause greater than self. There is this great scene in *The Hobbit* where Gandalf shows up at Bilbo's front door and says, "I am looking for someone to share in an adventure I am arranging, and it's very difficult to find anyone." Bilbo replies, "I should think so—in these parts! We are plain quiet folk and have no use for adventures. Nasty disturbing uncomfortable things! Make you late for dinner! I can't think what anybody sees in them." Thankfully, for all *Lord of the Rings* fans, Bilbo did eventually acquiesce, and a great adventure ensued.

Great leaders are always issuing invitations to a great adventure, I believe, but people often don't know that's what they want. They may have limited dreams, or dreams that are only about themselves, if they have any dreams at all. We must help people uncover their dreams, encourage their dreams, and provoke them to dream in line with God's good dreams for this broken world.

Marshall Goldsmith is one of the world's most respected leadership thinkers. I love his work and have learned much by reading him. I have a bone to pick, however—or perhaps a suggestion to make—regarding his revelation that part of the art of being a successful leadership consultant is to "discover someone's hot button. . . . If you press people to identify the motives behind their self-interest it usually boils down to four items: money, power, status and popularity." He does go on to say that people's hot buttons can change over time and that they can move to more legacy-leaving motivations, but even then it is still about self-interest.

I submit that each of us also has a hot button called "significance." Significance is what one experiences when a dream in one's head is connected to a dream in God's heart, and when that dream begins to be lived. Hospitable leaders know how to push that button. We make certain that we are encouraging the people we lead to make their dreams about more than their own self-interest. Really, I suppose this is in its own way ultimate self-interest:

> **Great leaders . . . must help people uncover their dreams, encourage their dreams, and provoke them to dream in line with God's good dreams for this broken world.**

Losing ourselves in a dream bigger than ourselves is the secret to fulfillment.

Those of us who have the privilege to lead can, like Jesus, be good shepherds—hospitable leaders—enthused to serve people with heads full of dreams and excited to challenge them to merge their dreams in an adventure that will last into eternity. This may sound all too esoteric and ethereal, but I believe every leader can get in on this. Each of us can ask how what we are leading is advancing good in this world. We can pay great attention to the good dreams in the people we lead. And we can accept responsibility to create environments where these people and their dreams can flourish in alignment with God's dreams for His world.

Leadership Take-Homes

1. **Hospitable leaders foster environments that encourage dreamers.** We must be intentional to cultivate—not to ignore nor crush—the dreams of those we lead.

2. **Hospitable leaders focus on the goals of the organization *and* on facilitating the dreams of the people who populate it.** We do not pursue our dreams at the expense of our followers.

3. **Connect your dreams to God's dreams.** Significance for hospitable leaders and followers comes in discovering and pursuing God's dreams for us, aligned with His good dreams for the world.

Sources

"was a balky and rather belligerent": Thomas Merton, *The Seven Storey Mountain* (Orlando: Harcourt, 1948), 69–70.

"you can see the change": Coldplay, "A Head Full of Dreams," by Guy
Berryman, Jonny Buckland, Will Champion, and Chris Martin, *A Head
Full of Dreams*, 2015, Parlophone/Atlantic Records.

"life in all its fullness": John 10:10 NCV.

"Jesus was in Jerusalem": John 10:22 NLT.

"Hanukkah thus became a season": Gary M. Burge, *NIV Application
Commentary on John* (Grand Rapids: Zondervan, 2000), 288.

"Woe to the shepherds of Israel": Ezekiel 34:2–10 NIV1984.

"mis-leaders. . . . the image of the leader will pass over": Eric Metaxas,
Bonhoeffer: Pastor, Martyr, Prophet, Spy (Nashville: Thomas Nelson,
2010), 141.

"A thief is only there to steal and kill": John 10:10–11 MESSAGE.

green pastures and quiet waters: Psalm 23.

"moral leaders inspire, influence and empower": Terry A. Smith, *Live 10:
Jump-Start the Best Version of Your Life* (Nashville: Thomas Nelson,
2013), 144–145.

"I was so overcome I could not stay myself": Steven Pressfield, *The Virtues
of War* (New York: Bantam, 2004), 5.

"five basic types of leadership": Richard Daft, *The Leadership Experience,*
2nd edition (Mason: Thomson, 2002), 441.

"life is essentially": David Brooks, *The Road to Character* (New York:
Random House, 2015), 262.

"leads Google's people function": Laszlo Bock, *Insights from Inside
Google: Work Rules!* (New York: Grand Central Publishing, 2015), 34, 38.

"I am looking for someone to share": J.R.R. Tolkien, *The Hobbit* (New
York: Houghton Mifflin Harcourt, 1937), 1.

"discover someone's hot button": Marshall Goldsmith, *What Got You Here
Won't Get You There* (New York: Hachette, 2007), 31, 32.

6

Anything Is Possible
in Your Area of Destiny

One of the great opportunities of hospitable leadership is the privilege of helping those we lead find their place in this world. A sense of place is essential to being at home with oneself and with God and to feeling at home in the cosmos. When Richard Foster wrote about the unique contribution of Pseudo-Dionysius (ca. AD 500) to the development of Christian thought regarding the right ordering of the universe, he penned that Dionysus underscored "the importance of place in our world." Foster added, "We cannot be 'placeless.' As long as we are finite human beings we need a place, a role, a function in life. Placeless human beings are among the most miserable in our day."

Hospitable leadership is differentiated from other kinds of leadership emphases in that hospitable leaders are particularly obsessed with helping followers find their place. We are not only hospitable to people with heads full of dreams; we are also dream refiners. We are insistent that people develop clarity about the life God dreams specifically for them.

Roman Oben is a good friend of mine and a longtime member of the congregation I serve. Roman had a great career in the NFL as an offensive tackle, including winning Super Bowl XXXVII with the Tampa Bay Buccaneers. After he retired from the NFL, he experienced what a lot of former professional athletes face after retirement: a sense of placelessness. He found himself trying to figure out who he was now that he was not playing. What—at least professionally—was he supposed to do with the rest of his life? What new dreams should he dream and pursue? He had significant opportunities as a commentator in radio and television but did not ultimately feel like that was his place. Roman and I had several discussions about his new journey, and during this time he began facilitating a class around my book, *Live 10*, in which considerable energy is spent trying to help people find their place, or what I call Area of Destiny.

> Hospitable leaders are particularly obsessed with helping followers find their place.

Here's part of an email Roman sent me that describes some of his process around dream refinement. He says it better than I can.

"Hey man! I just wanted to thank you for that meeting we had . . . where I shared the vision of what I wanted to do with my career paths. . . . It seems like every time I teach a Live 10 course at the main campus, I always get to intimately know a wonderful group of people, while also discovering a lot about myself in the process. . . . For years I've been struggling to make a greater impact in society than anything I ever did on the football field—if at all, my career was more of an impact on me and my family's experiences than society as a whole. Starting in 2008 doing postgame radio for the Giants, then 2011 transitioning to TV, I was able to transition that into discussing topics about sports as they affect the bigger picture on national news shows. But I didn't believe that was what God intended for my future.

It's been a huge passion of mine to give back to the game of football what it did for me, and help grow the game and lead the next generation of players and fans. When I was asked by the commissioner and league front office to interview for this position as Director of Youth/High School Football, I knew that God had finally presented the opportunity that I've been praying for. A leadership position in the business of sports that helps meet and advance the future needs of our game is a big task, but we serve a much bigger God. . . . You're the man! Boom!"

Soon after I received this email, SportsIllustrated.com ran a headline over a gigantic picture of Roman that announced, "The Man in Charge of the Future of Football." Roman is now the NFL's vice president of Youth Football. Very little that I do fires me up more than hearing a story like this. It has nothing to do with Roman's celebrity but everything to do with helping people discover the life God dreams for them in line with His dreams for His world. To find their place and to be at home in the cosmos.

Old Testament scholar John H. Walton writes that the essence of the Hebrew word for *created* in the Genesis story "concerns bringing heaven and earth into existence and focuses on operation through the assignment of roles and functions." He connects this to the work of God "*in the fixing of destinies.*" God designed us so that when we find our place in this world and do what we were made to do, we experience a deeply satisfying sense of destiny fulfillment. People have an insatiable need to know what their role and function is in the operation of this world, and leaders have a wonderful opportunity to satisfy this "I'm trying to find my place" angst that many people live with every day. This is what helping people discover their Area of Destiny is all about. We must each find that place where we connect to our fixed destiny.

I believe that helping people discover their Area of Destiny is one of the most important things I can do as a leader. Area of Destiny is a life-organizing principle. It is a way of understanding our individual life in the bigger picture of the world. Area of Destiny describes the God-defined boundaries—and possibilities—of my life. It is my place, the context in which I am to live and love and work and play. It encompasses all dimensions of my life: relationships, vocation, avocations, assignments, and possibilities. It usually—but not always—includes a specific geography.

Our place is about much more than where we live though. Area of Destiny is the predestined framework of my life. The apostle Paul alluded to this kind of thinking when he wrote to the Corinthians that he "will not boast beyond proper limits but will confine our boasting to the sphere of service God himself has assigned to us," and when he spoke to the Athenians and declared "God began by making one person, and from him came all the different people who live everywhere in the world. God decided exactly when and where they must live."

Here is what is so extremely important to me: Within our Area of Destiny, there is limitless possibility. I disagree strongly with those well-intentioned folks who say that we can be anything we want to be and do anything we want to do anywhere we want to do it. I would rather say that we can do anything we were made to do, wherever we were made to do it. I believe that when God created us, He assigned us a role, a function, a place where we connect with our destiny.

To play our assigned role does not mean that we are preprogrammed automatons. Part of God's will is that we exercise our will, and that includes making choices about how to live our lives and actualize possibilities within our Area of Destiny. I like very much that Dallas Willard taught, "We can be solidly in the will of God, and know that we are, without knowing God's preference with regard to various details of our lives. We can be in his will as we do certain things without our knowing that he prefers those actions to certain other possibilities. . . . Generally, we are in God's will whenever we are leading the kind of life he wants for us."

It is amazing to witness the incredible freedom people experience when they believe they are living the life they were meant to live. As Os Guinness wrote, "The truth is not that God is finding a place for our gifts but that God has created us and our gifts for a place of his choosing—and we will only be ourselves when we are finally there." It thrills me that not only can I inspire people to dream but that I can also help them dream within their God-destined place.

Russ Hammonds is a hospitable dad and a really smart guy. Though he is now a very successful producer of television programming (an Area of Destiny thing for him), he has a degree in physics from Brown University. He likes to understand how things work. His nine-year-old daughter is precocious and unusually inquisitive. Inquisitive enough to ask her dad to explain Area of Destiny. So he drew a Venn diagram for her. In one circle he wrote the word *Mission*. In another he wrote *Passion*. And in a third circle he wrote *Gifts*. And in the area where the three circles intersect he wrote *Destiny*. He told his daughter that Area of Destiny is the intersection of Mission, Passion, and Gifts. I think he got it exactly right.

Mission asks questions such as, "What are God's dreams for His world?" "What role do I feel called to play in His mission?" "Where am I needed?" *Passion* begs questions like, "What good things do I love to do?" Or put another way, "In what meaningful activities do I feel pleasure?" *Gifts* should focus us on discovering the talents we have been given for service—the things we are particularly good at—and taking action to develop those gifts into skills that could allow us to make a unique contribution.

This nine-year-old girl gave her dad's explanation of Area of Destiny some serious thought. The next day she wrote on a Post-it Note her take on her place in this world—at least in terms of vocation. "Work against racial and sexul (sic) segregation in STEM fields." Her dad's interpretation of this is that she wants to work against race and gender segregation in STEM fields. My guess is that this sense of place will be refined many times as she grows older. But imagine being nine years old and thinking with such intentionality about your life.

I suggest that leaders (like Russ and his wife, Lauren) should constantly challenge those they lead—in this case, one's children—to insist on living the life they were created to live. Area of Destiny is about more than vocation. It's discovering what our lives are supposed to be about and organizing everything in our lives accordingly. Everything in our lives should be put to this test: "Is this—whatever I am dreaming, thinking, planning, doing—in sync with my God-destined place in this world?" Possibility and fulfillment live here.

This way of leadership—helping people find their place—requires a certain unselfishness. Back in the fifth century John Cassian wrote in *The Conferences* that avarice, or greed, is the root of inhospitality. If we are to be hospitable to people and their dreams, we simply cannot be selfish. Frankly, this has been difficult for me at times. I have big dreams and I want as many people as possible to join me in fulfilling what I believe are my God-inspired dreams. Thankfully, over the years there have been many, many wonderful people in my life who believe that part of their place in this world is to help my dreams come true.

And then there are many wonderful people who have left what I am doing to go do what I helped inspire them to do elsewhere. In this I'm reminded of Augustine, who loved to be surrounded by his friends in vocational ministry, but who found himself in middle age lonely at times, as many of his intimates had been sent to pursue their callings far away from Hippo in North Africa, where Augustine lived. "But when you yourself begin to surrender some of the very dearest and sweetest of those you have reared, to the needs of churches situated far from you, then you will understand the pangs of longing that stab me on losing the physical presence of friends, united to me in the most close and sweet intimacy." There are times when the price of hospitable leadership is this feeling of being "stabbed," when someone you love and have partnered with decides their place no longer intersects with your place. This is just part of the deal though, when one aspect of our dream is to help our followers' dreams come true, in their God-destined place.

In Isak Dinesen's classic short story "The Roads Round Pisa," a sophisticated and well-traveled guest is asked by his host, "What does a guest want?" The answer is fascinating and wise: "A guest wants first of all to be diverted, to get out of his daily monotony or worry. Secondly the decent guest wants to shine, to expand himself and impress his own personality upon his surroundings. And thirdly, perhaps, he wants to find some justification for his existence altogether." Much could be said about this. I want to focus on the desire of the guest to "expand himself, and impress his own personality upon his surrounding."

We must make certain that in every possible leadership setting we are creating space for those we lead to expand themselves. This is not only about paying attention to their dreams but also being hospitable to the gifts they bring, listening to their ideas, giving them room to be creative, allowing them to make critical decisions, and providing opportunities for them to grow. And sometimes . . . to go. Henri Nouwen nails this point, as he does so many other facets of hospitality. He noted that "the paradox of hospitality is that it wants to create . . . a friendly emptiness where strangers can enter and discover themselves as created free; free to sing their own songs, speak their own languages, dance their own dances; free also to leave and follow their own vocations. Hospitality is not a subtle invitation to adopt the lifestyle of the host, but the gift of a chance for the guest to find his own."

> **Hospitable leaders are not interested in creating people in our image. We are interested in creating space for people to become who they were made to be.**

Hospitable leaders are not interested in creating people in our image. We are interested in creating space for people to become who they were made to be. To find their place and to be everything they were meant to be in that place.

Nouwen applies this principle to the relationship between parents and children: "Our children are our most important guests, who enter into our home, ask for careful attention, stay for a while and then leave to follow their own way." He goes on to remind us that the temptation is to "cling to our children to use them for our own unfulfilled needs and to hold on to them. . . ." But we must remember that they are guests in our home, that they have their own destination, which we need to help them find. And when they do, everything in our beings should rejoice that they have their place in this world, wherever that place may be.

I believe this way of thought and practice should mark our approach toward those we lead in every arena, with this caveat: Though our children will at some point—hopefully!—leave our physical home and stewardship, I do not believe that everyone we lead, or even most everyone we lead, must or should leave our leadership sphere in order to follow their own dreams.

In most circumstances, for leaders to be successful, we must be surrounded by people whose dreams are connected with ours. It is not selfish for us to want that, and even to encourage it. Thankfully, as I have already expressed, over the years I have been blessed with many people who have found their place in my place. It is impossible for a leader to do great things without a collaborative commitment by great groups to do terrific things together.

We must create an environment where those who are expanded by going are sent with our blessings, but also where those who feel called to stay can expand as well. Sometimes this is more challenging than saying good-bye. Those who stay—who we say hello to again and again—must be given room to impress themselves on their surroundings, to refer to Dinesen's words again. We must make room for driven, talented, creative people to dream . . . and stay. To be a part of something they did not create perhaps, but to be able to help create a shared future in partnership with leaders who are hospitable to dreamers and their dreams.

In an intersect of parental and pastoral leadership, my son Christian—our youngest—has expressed that he feels called to join me and the other leaders of our church to help us lead our congregation into our future. I have been lead pastor here for twenty-six years as of this writing. He is twenty-five. His entire life has been wrapped up in this place. I couldn't be more excited. Or in a way, challenged. He is intelligent, well-studied, creative, and full of sanctified ambition. He has a strong leadership gift and is developing into an outstanding communicator. One of my greatest responsibilities, in my view, is to make certain that there is room in this place for him to find his place, and to be able to fully expand . . . here. I thrill to this challenge. I will work hard to make certain that his dreams can flourish in this place where my dreams have flourished all these years.

Our daughter, Sumerr, our oldest, is not involved in vocational ministry. She has a special gift to nurture children and cares for them professionally and feels called to have lots of children on her own, and to raise them to live the lives God dreamed for them. She is a delightful girl with a personality that lights up the room and a heart that is full of desire to do good in this world. Thankfully, she has decided to make her home close to our home. I will do everything in my power to play whatever role she asks me to play in her life, to cheer her on and more, as she pursues God's designs for her life in her own way and in her unique place. I'm glad she will be close to home. There is plenty of room for her here.

And then there is our middle child, Caleb. He has already been mentioned several times in this book for whatever reason, which will ensure that he will be teased vociferously by his siblings. Caleb has chosen to pursue his dreams elsewhere—far away from home. He believes that his Area of Destiny includes writing and making movies and acting, and that in order to be successful at this—which he already is—he needs to live in Los Angeles. And though, like Augustine, I feel the "pangs of longing that stab me" when I see his seat empty at our table, I couldn't be happier. I'm sure you understand why by now. He has found his place in this world. And to a hospitable leader, that's ultimately what matters. My responsibility is to be hospitable to people and their dreams, wherever that may take them. I simply must help them find the place where their God-inspired dreams can come true.

Leadership Take-Homes

1. **One of the most important roles of the hospitable leader is to help followers identify and operate in their Area of Destiny.** Only when someone is living in the intersection of their mission, passion, and gifts can they truly live their best life.

2. **We must help people succeed in their God-destined place in this world.** The hospitable leader should continually challenge those they lead to live the life for which they were created.

3. **A hospitable leader is an unselfish leader.** We must lead people to expand and grow within our sphere of leadership and from our sphere of leadership.

Sources

"the importance of place": Richard Foster, *Longing for God: Seven Paths of Christian Devotion* (Downers Grove: InterVarsity Press, 2009), 246–247.

"Hey man!": Roman Oben, email communication with Terry Smith.

"concerns bringing heaven and earth": John H. Walton, *Genesis: The NIV Application Commentary* (Grand Rapids: Zondervan, 2001), 72.

"would not boast beyond proper": 2 Corinthians 10:13.

"God began by making one person": Acts 17:26 NCV.

"We can be solidly in the will": Dallas Willard, *Hearing God: Developing a Conversational Relationship with God* (Downers Grove: InterVarsity Press, 2012), 13.

"The truth is not that God": Os Guinness, *The Call: Finding and Fulfilling the Central Purpose of Your Life* (Nashville: Thomas Nelson, 1998), 46.

Area of Destiny is about more than vocation.: Nine-year-old's Post-it Note to her father, Russ Hammonds.

My friends Jack and Suzy Welch have made a significant contribution to the Area of Destiny concept. See their book *The Real Life MBA: Your No-BS Guide to Winning the Game, Building a Team, and Growing Your Career* (New York: Harper Collins, 2015).

Avarice, or greed, is the root of inhospitality: John Cassian, *The Conferences* (Mahwah: Paulist Press, 1997), 198.

"But when you yourself begin to surrender": Augustine, as quoted by Peter Brown in *Augustine of Hippo: A Biography* (Berkeley and Los Angeles, CA: University of California Press, 2000), 197.

"Pisa . . . What does a guest want?": Isak Dinesen, "The Roads Round Pisa," *Seven Gothic Tales* (New York: Vintage, 1972), 185.

"the paradox of hospitality": Henri Nouwen, *Reaching Out* (New York: Doubleday, 1986), 72, 81–84.

"pangs of longing that stab me": Augustine, as quoted by Brown in *Augustine of Hippo*, 197.

7

Dream Challenge

A leader with great dreams is going to face great challenges. And a leader who inspires others to dream great dreams is going to be *surrounded by people* who are facing great challenges. Dreamers have to fight to see their dreams come true.

Several years ago, while leading my congregation through a time-, money-, and energy-consuming building project, I began to experience chest pains. Initial medical tests showed some cause for concern so I was prescribed a battery of more extensive tests to make sure that my heart was okay. One of these tests—a nuclear stress test of some sort—happened to be in a medical office building next door to the land we were preparing to build on. I say "preparing to build," because though we were several years and several million dollars into this project, all that had physically happened to that point was some of the site preparation. It turned out that an incredible amount of time and resources had to be spent just to blast and remove the massive rock formations hiding just under the surface of the ground.

Our experts had warned us there would be some blasting necessary, but no one knew the extent of this challenge until the work got underway, and then month after month, every workday was déjà vu: dynamite drilled into place, roaring explosions, massive clouds of dust or mud filling the air, rumbling bulldozers—and more than one hundred dump trucks loudly entering the construction site, being filled with rock, backfiring their way off the property and back to whence they came. Did I mention that this cost a lot of money? And all we had for our effort was an obnoxiously unsightly, chaotically disarranged, murkily muddy hole in the ground that got larger by the day. And did I mention I was having chest pains?

So I'm walking on a treadmill in the medical office building next to this ongoing project, shot full of some dye and with electrodes hooked up all over my chest. I exercise regularly enough that it was taking some time for my heart rate to elevate enough for the test to be effective. As the technician kept raising the incline and pace of the treadmill, I could tell he was getting a little frustrated with my continued low heart rate. Finally he said, "Let's open this blind," and pointed to a window that I had been blankly staring at as I walked. I was disoriented in the office building and was oblivious to what this window faced. But when the tech pulled the cord and the blind rapidly rolled up, I found myself staring at that gigantic, ugly, and very expensive hole in the ground next door. Our project. Then the technician yelled, "Something is wrong! His heart rate just shot up. We have to stop this test and make sure he's okay." Of course, at that point I didn't need a doctor to diagnose my problem. That project I was staring at was a pain in my . . . chest.

This project represented a huge dream. I had inspired a whole lot of people to dream big with me. They had stepped out in radical faith and sacrificed significantly. We were all in. But at that point I felt like I had just led us all into a big, muddy— and did I mention expensive?—mess. As with most dreams I have had, I just hadn't realized how hard actualizing the dream would be.

Through experiences like this—and many other stress-inducing adventures—I have suffered enough dream-making angina by now to have some sense of what it costs to pursue something great. I know if I have a worthy vision I will face prodigious resistance. It's like all the powers of this world and the dark world align themselves to stop dreamers and their dreams. This is just the way things are in this present age. I get it.

But let's take this to another level: It's one thing for me to suffer through the inevitable and immense challenges of dream making; it's another thing for me to witness the heartache of the people around me whom I have inspired to dream, and helped to refine their dreams, and provoked to go after their dreams. It's one thing for me to have a pain in *my* chest; it's another for me to know that I am, at least in part, the reason a whole lot of the people I lead have a proverbial pain in *their* chest as well.

Frankly, when I think about experiences like I had on that treadmill, I wonder why I would ever want anyone else, especially the people I love and lead, to suffer through seasons like that. But if I am hospitable to people and their dreams, this is part of what I know will happen. I will always be surrounded by people who are suffering to see their dreams come true.

So what do we do? Well, stop whining already, for one. (I wrote that to myself.) Now that the resistance and the painful part of dream making is acknowledged, it's time to get on with it.

Every leader needs a little Winston Churchill in them. He of the "I have nothing to offer but blood, toil, tears and sweat, but the cause is great and we are going to win, and it's going to be worth it" leadership school. One evening in 1945, after rallying the free world to fight and win the Second World War, Churchill was at dinner when a woman at the table asked, "Now that it is all over, what was your worst moment in the war—the fall of France, the threat of the invasion, the Blitz?" After a minute he answered, "Frankly, my dear, I enjoyed every moment of it." He essentially said that he enjoyed the fight. Now, did he really enjoy sleeping on a cot in his underground war room listening to bombs fall on London above him during the blitzkrieg? Did he really enjoy the heartrending tribulations and terrors of war? I doubt it. But he was glad to be involved in a great cause—standing against evil—and shaping history. He embraced the fight, challenged his nation to fight, and led the free world to victory.

I don't know how many times I have had people come up to me and say something like, "You inspired me to start a new business," or go back to school, or run for the school board, or launch a nonprofit, or ask her to marry me—and I think, *Yes!* And then they will say, "My new business is really struggling, and I hope we're going to make it through this next quarter," or some similar thing. And my heart drops and I am tempted to say, "I'm sorry I inspired you." Really. But instead I say something like, "I'm sorry you are struggling . . . but you have to relish the fight. God will use this to shape you. Isn't this battle better than living an uninspired status-quo life? You are going to make it. Don't lose the faith. Your struggle now will make the victory sweeter in your future. Someday this will make a great story. I am praying for you."

I have thought many times about this Scripture in the Old Testament book of Judges—or Leaders: "Now these are the nations which the Lord left, that He might test Israel by them, that is, all who had not known any of the wars in Canaan (this was only so that the generations of the children of Israel might be taught to know war, at least those who had not formerly known it)." The people of Israel had finally been led into the

Promised Land and had fought long and hard to secure it. But God made sure they still had some enemies left to fight. Why? Because they needed something to fight for. This was especially true for new generations of leaders who had not been engaged in the battles and the setbacks and the victories of the past. One paraphrase of this passage states that "God wanted to give opportunity to the youth of Israel to exercise faith and obedience in conquering their enemies."

This passage—about physical and literal events in history, and specific to the time and people it was written for—points to a larger life principle demonstrated throughout all of Scripture: If God loves us, He will give us something great to fight for. Thomas Merton asserted, "Souls are like athletes, that need opponents worthy of them, if they are to be tried and extended and pushed to the full use of their powers, and rewarded according to their capacity."

I sometimes hear leaders say something along the lines of, "I sacrificed so you won't have to." I especially hear well-meaning parents say this. And I get it. But if you love the people you are leading, you will inspire them to have vision and dream dreams and take risks, which they will have to suffer for. This is true on a corporate level of course. An organization always has to have a dream so big that it demands new generations of stakeholders to struggle to achieve it. And it's also true for individuals. We can never be satisfied with only the thing we already fought for. There is always more to be done. More possibility to embrace. More of our Area of Destiny to actualize. We *need* to be fully engaged—and to challenge those we lead to be fully engaged—in the struggle for a good and great cause. We need to constantly incite people to have a dream worth fighting for.

In his inimitable style, Steven Pressfield wrote of a general who rewarded some in his army who had distinguished themselves in battle with gifts or inclusion at his table. "But to those he wished most to esteem, he sent not boons but trials.

He singled them out for the most perilous duties, for in these, he said, he sent out lieutenants and got back captains." We are not doing those we lead a favor when we protect them from difficult assignments. I think we make a grave mistake when we buy in to the understandable but misguided notion that good leaders should make everything as easy as possible for everyone around them. If we do this, we deny the people we are leading the perquisites of struggle and sacrifice— the glory of the battle—and the advancement that follows.

> If you love the people you are leading, you will inspire them to have vision and dream dreams and take risks, which they will have to suffer for.

I love the language Teddy Roosevelt used to describe some of his formative— and difficult—years as a rancher and deputy sheriff in the cold frontier of North Dakota. "We knew toil and hardship and hunger and thirst; and we saw men die violent deaths as they worked among the horses and the cattle, or fought in evil feuds with one another; but we felt the beat of hardy life in our veins, and ours was the glory of work and the joy of living." This kind of sentiment, about the efficacy of struggle, needs to inform the way we challenge people to approach their lives. There always needs to be a new frontier, a great cause, where our character is tested and revealed and more fully formed, where we must rely on God and grace, where we can win great victories, and be promoted to more and more meaningful responsibilities.

A hospitable leader should love people so much, and want them to live a full and abundant life so passionately that we create environments, present opportunities, and issue challenges that welcome the difficulties inherent in dream fulfillment. We are in a great moral struggle. We are called to advance good in this world. We each have a specific assignment in this conflict.

We must not get "wobbly" as Churchill might have said. We should run to the battle and challenge those we lead to do the same.

I have always been fascinated with the way the apostle Paul remonstrated his young ministry partner and protégé Timothy in the letters he wrote to him that we call First and Second Timothy. Timothy was a nineteen-year-old young man when Paul recognized something special in him and invited him to be part of his leadership team. Timothy traveled with Paul until he was about thirty years old. And then, in AD 64, Paul gave him a very difficult assignment. Paul asked him—commanded him, actually—to stay in Ephesus, a large metropolitan area in Asia Minor, present-day Turkey. Timothy was tasked with the critical responsibility of fighting against false teaching that was being propagated in the nascent Christian church there and threatening the Ephesian church's survival. And he was charged to raise up leaders who would stabilize this church. This was a pivotal moment in early Christianity.

Timothy appears to have been challenged beyond his natural capabilities in this assignment, which occasioned Paul's first letter to him. Paul begins this letter by urging Timothy to stay in Ephesus. Why did he have to urge him to stay there? Because Timothy wanted to leave. He had a tough assignment and he wanted out.

Everything we know about Timothy indicates that his natural disposition was one of some timidity. He was given to anxiety. He seems to have been easily pushed around, discouraged, even depressed. He had a nervous stomach, was intimidated in the presence of older leaders, and fearful in new places. A central passage in Paul's correspondence to him sums up Paul's challenge to Timothy—at least in the context of his assignment in Ephesus: "For this reason I remind you to fan into flame the gift of God, which is in you through the laying on of my hands. For the Spirit God gave us does not make us timid, but gives us power, love and self-discipline." The Expositor's Greek Testament renders it "your weak point is a deficiency in moral courage." Ouch.

I specify that these apparently harsh words were a part of Paul's message to Timothy in the context of Ephesus. Timothy's body of work prior to his Ephesian assignment is more than impressive. He had already represented Paul and done indispensable work over several years in three churches in three major cities; Thessalonica in AD 50, Corinth in AD 53 through 54, and Philippi in AD 60 through 62. Timothy had collaborated with Paul in six of his letters that we know of, which are now a part of the New Testament. Remember that early Christianity is arguably the most significant movement in the history of humanity, and that the New Testament has been and is the most read—and in many people's views, the most important—literature in history. Timothy played a key role in this. The leadership lessons here are rich and relevant today.

Paul loved Timothy. A lot. He valued him in ways impossible to fully articulate. He called Timothy his beloved and faithful son. He wrote to the Philippians, "I have no one else like him . . . Timothy has proved himself." Yet when he wrote directly to Timothy in Ephesus, Paul got in his face: Stay there and do what you have been assigned to do. Don't be intimidated. Don't give in to your natural weaknesses. Stir up the gifts of God that are in you. Remember who you really are. You can do this, Timothy. You must do this.

The Ephesian assignment exposed Timothy's weak points. Regardless of his past success, here was a new frontier that challenged every part of who he was. And Paul had put him in this position. Was Paul a hospitable leader when he gave Timothy this assignment that was so difficult that it apparently pushed him to a breaking point? Was he a good leader when he got in

Timothy's face and challenged him to rise to this new occasion? I think so. He loved Timothy so much that he gave him a cause to fight for, in line with God's call on his life, that would build him and build his faith and allow him to live knowing that he had fulfilled his destiny. "This charge I commit to you, son Timothy, according to the prophecies previously made concerning you, that by them you may wage the good warfare, having faith and a good conscience." Paul saw more in Timothy than Timothy saw in himself, and he challenged him to lose himself in a cause greater than himself, for the sake of the mission and for Timothy's own self-actualization.

Timothy rose to this challenge. It's intriguing to me that when Paul wrote his second letter to Timothy, it was in part a request for him to leave Ephesus and to come and visit him in Rome. Paul was in prison for preaching the Good News about Jesus, and he knew he was about to be executed. And Timothy was the person he wanted at his side. In Paul's first letter to Timothy he urged him to stay in Ephesus, fulfill his charge, and fight the battle well. In his second letter he wrote in part, "Do your best to come to me quickly. . . . Do your best to get here before winter."

We do not know if Timothy ever made it to Rome. Most likely he did not. What history does indicate is that Timothy stayed in Ephesus and became the first bishop of the Christian church there. It appears that he was martyred in Ephesus some thirty years after Paul's death in Rome. It is sad to think that Paul died without seeing his spiritual son again. But my guess is that Paul died proud. Timothy had found his place, even though at first he didn't want to be there. Paul, however, knew. He knew this Ephesian assignment would bring out the best in Timothy. Like any good leader, he dreamed more for Timothy than Timothy had even dreamed for himself.

Sometimes my heart just aches when I see someone I love—who I inspired to dream or challenged to take on a difficult assignment—suffer through some of the same things I have suffered through over the years. I wish I could protect them from the pain that pulses through any attempt to do something great. Then I remember that I want them to have the same sense of immense satisfaction I feel when I drive up to a majestic building standing on the property that once was just a big, muddy, expensive hole in the ground . . . and a pain in my chest.

And that's just a building project.

Much more than that, the unmitigated joy I feel at the lives I have seen changed because God gave me—and gives me—consequential dreams and demanding assignments, surpasses any sense of struggle I have ever experienced. I do not want to deny anyone I lead the ineffable depth of fulfillment that can only be tasted when someone has a dream significant enough that they must fight to make the dream come true. Challenging people to want something worthy enough to struggle for is one of the most hospitable things a leader can do.

> **Challenging people to want something worthy enough to struggle for is one of the most hospitable things a leader can do.**

And then there is encouragement. I have stressed the need to challenge people because I don't think this kind of challenge is usually associated with "hospitable leader." But I should say that most of the time I issue challenges in the language of encouragement.

To encourage means to intensify courage. The prefix "en" before "courage" is an intensifier. Hospitable leaders dare people to fight for their dreams and then encourage them like crazy when they do.

I have been thinking about the Twenty-Third Psalm in this light. The psalmist wrote that the Good Shepherd prepared a table for him in the presence of his enemies. This describes "a banquet hall where a gracious host provides lavish hospitality."

Sadly, whenever there is a dream there is opposition. If I am doing my job right I will be surrounded by dreamers who will at times feel surrounded by trouble in the midst of the fight to advance good and beautiful things in this world. So I must be careful to be a good shepherd who provides lavish hospitality even—and especially—in the presence of all the difficulties dreamers face.

I think about this sometimes when I prepare to speak to my congregation on a Sunday morning. Here are all these people with their heads and hearts full of dreams. I try to focus on the fact that like me, they experience seasons when it feels like they are in an all-out war, battling to see their dreams come true. And I try to prepare a table for them in the presence of their enemies—trials and setbacks and woundings and heartbreaks and suffering. It's as if I invite them to sit down and have a feast in the middle of this big muddy mess. I encourage them: "It's going to be more than okay. If God is for you, who can be against you? Embrace the fight! The victory will make the struggle worth it. You'll see . . . your God-inspired dreams are going to come true."

Leadership Take-Homes

1. **With big dreams comes big resistance.** The God who loves us gives us something great to fight for.

2. **Embrace the glory of battle.** Hospitable leaders do not make everything easy for their followers, but rather allow them to enjoy struggle and sacrifice and the advancement that follows.

3. **Challenge + Encouragement = Growth.** We must offer growth challenges in the language of encouragement and provide a lavish feast of support as those we lead face the difficulties of making dreams reality.

Sources

"I have nothing to offer": Winston Churchill, *Blood, Toil, Tears and Sweat Speech*, 1940, May 13, www.winstonchurchill.org/resources/speeches/1940-the-finest-hour/blood-toil-tears-and-sweat-2/ (as prime minister).

"Now that it is all over": Jon Meacham, *Franklin and Winston: Intimate Portrait of an Epic Friendship* (New York: Random House, 2004), 14.

"Now these are the nations": Judges 3:1–2 NKJV.

"God wanted to give opportunity": Judges 3:1–2 TLB.

"Souls are like athletes": Thomas Merton, *The Seven Storey Mountain* (Wilmington: Mariner Books, 1999), 92.

"But to those he wished most": Steven Pressfield, *Tides of War: A Novel of Alcibiades and the Peloponnesian War* (New York: Bantam, 2001), 258.

"We knew toil and hardship and hunger": Edmund Morris, *Colonel Roosevelt* (New York: Random House, 2010), 267.

Paul urging Timothy to stay in Ephesus: 1 Timothy 1:3.

"For this reason": 2 Timothy 1:6–7.

"your weak point is a deficiency": W. Nicoll Robertson, et. al. *The Expositor's Greek Testament* (New York: Dodd Mead, 1910), 152.

faithful son: 1 Corinthians 4:17.

"I have no one else": Philippians 2:20, 22.

"This charge I commit to you": 1 Timothy 1:18–19 NKJV.

"Do your best to come to me quickly.": 2 Timothy 4:9.

"Do your best to get here before winter.": 2 Timothy 4:21.

"a banquet hall": John F. Walvoord and Roy B. Zuck, *The Bible Knowledge Commentary: Old Testament* (Colorado Springs: David C. Cook, 1983), 812.

COMMUNICATION

8

Grace and Truth

Hospitable leaders establish communicative climates in which truth can be spoken . . . and hopefully received. If we love ourselves and want to grow, and if we love the people we lead and want them to grow, we must not reduce hospitality to a bland sentimentality. I suggest rather that we learn to practice *hospitable communication*. Hospitable communication is the reciprocal sharing of who we really are and what we really think, in loving environments and in loving ways, to promote one another's growth.

I was inspired many years ago when I read an article by organizational leadership expert Rodney Ferris, in which he advocated "organizational love." "I propose that love be made an acceptable, if not essential, component of leadership. . . . I believe that the manifestation of love is the secret to increased productivity and organizational effectiveness," he wrote. But Ferris did not suggest creating an easy environment for leaders or those they lead. He went on to say that organizational love also means "telling employees where they stand with compassion (tough love) . . . Love is concerned with being honest, first with yourself and then with others. It's not easy to tell someone a painful truth; on the other hand, if that telling is seen as a loving, learning experience for both of you, the anticipated pain can become a mutually beneficial bond."

The apostle Paul would certainly have agreed with this. He intimated to the Ephesians that truth must be spoken in love so people can grow.

I like this idea of an organizational culture so infused with love that even the most difficult things can be said—and dealt with—in an honest way that promotes the growth of everyone concerned and the organization itself. Hospitable leaders create space for truth. This is the only way positive change can occur in the life of an individual. It is the only way to achieve true reconciliation between God and people, and between people and people. It is the only way to raise healthy children. It is the only way to have intimacy in a marriage. It is the only way to advance mission in holistically healthy ways. It is the only way to lead people to ultimate Truth.

We do not need to make a false choice between love and truth. God communicated himself to the world through Jesus, who is "full of grace and truth." One without the other is wholly ineffective. Jesus displayed this through His life and leadership. He was incredibly gracious—hospitable—but not at all afraid to speak even the most difficult truth. He said that the truth would set us free.

Elizabeth Newman reminds us that "Jesus' inclusivity is not without expectations." This is demonstrated in the story of the woman who was caught in adultery. Jesus showed profound grace when He accepted her, and dissuaded the judgmental legalists who had caught her in this sin from stoning her: "Let any one of you who is without sin be the first to throw a stone at her." Yet He loved her so much that He called her to a different way of life: "Go now and leave your life of sin." Grace alone makes us feel better only for a little while. It's the truth, wrapped in grace, that helps us become who we were meant to be.

The challenge for so many of us who are inclined to a hospitable leadership is that we are often and understandably hesitant to say the hard thing. Perhaps we are afraid we will sound like Jack Nicholson in the movie *A Few Good Men*, who thunders at an ostensibly naïve Tom Cruise, "You can't handle the truth!" If you are at all like me, you care about people so much that you worry a difficult truth will not offer them welcome but rather run them away. I disdain tough conversations with my wife, children, staff, or congregants. Sometimes it's the discomfort I feel when truth is spoken to me about me, and that challenges me to get better. But frankly, that is not as trying for me as when I need to speak honestly about anything that might bring growth pains to someone I love. However, as M. Scott Peck so brilliantly confronted us, "To fail to confront when confrontation is required for the nurture of spiritual growth represents a failure to love equally as does thoughtless criticism or condemnation and other forms of active deprivation of caring."

It's the truth, wrapped in grace, that helps us become who we were meant to be.

Scripture teaches us that "love . . . rejoices with the truth." We must each figure out how to get love and truth to rejoice together in our leadership context.

Thankfully, hospitality offers us the possibility of creating environments where people are willing to listen to one another, even when listening challenges us to our core.

Some time ago I tackled a subject in a sermon that was very controversial in terms of the larger societal conversation. I felt I needed to do this in order to address questions my congregants were asking and to be faithful to my calling as a Christian pastor. As I stood in the lobby and greeted people afterward, a couple came up and introduced themselves. They were first-time guests. He is the producer of a very highly rated national television talk show famous in part for humorously disparaging people with a point of view similar to the one I had just espoused. He said, "I disagree with nearly everything you said today. But I respect that you said it and appreciate the way you said it." They have become regular attenders since that day. Still disagreeing on some points, no doubt, but still listening. They know that I love them. That I will hear them. That I respect them and their right to hold views antithetical to what I believe to be true. That they are welcome.

The key to speaking truth that has the potential to be received and that promotes positive change and growth is to create an environment where we listen and speak in a way that encourages people to listen to us. In his wonderful book *Leadership Communication*, Richard L. Stoppe suggests that "Communicative climate is as important to emotional life as the weather is to physical life. Communicatively, climate describes qualities such as trust, love, provisionalism, acceptance, active listening, empathetic understanding, positive attitudes, recognition, and respect."

In my experience, it's amazing what you can say to people when they know you love them and when you convey your message hospitably. A chief technology officer at one of the largest firms on Wall Street told me that this hospitality paradigm has changed the way in which he fires people. He tells me that when it is necessary to dismiss people, he does it from a genuine perspective of love for them. He really wants what is best for them and the organization he serves. He has conversations with them about their lives and gifts and passions. He helps them understand why they are not the best fit for his organization. He encourages them into their future and does everything in his power to help them land on their feet. He now fires people hospitably, if you please. And he tells me that this has made a meaningful difference in this most difficult of experiences for him and for the people he is trying to love through a hard transition.

I know that loving people—even those you have to let go—is not necessarily rocket science. But thinking about it in this way was a significant paradigm shift for this powerful CTO. He is becoming a more hospitable leader in the crazy world of Wall Street. I think that's a pretty good place to strive for practical implementation of organizational love and hospitable communication.

The need to create safe places where truth can be spoken and heard is one of the most important responsibilities of a hospitable leader. I am thinking about truth here in two ways. One is the claim of Jesus to be the Truth and the mandate Christ-followers have to promulgate this truth and the life-giving truths of Scripture. From my perspective, this speaks to an objective truth that must be clearly communicated even when it might appear people have no desire to listen. I am also thinking about truth as it concerns our own more personal and subjective truths. What we think and feel and believe—that which is true to us, but which does not rise to the level of objective truth. It's appropriate—and necessary—for us to be able to communicate out of who we are about things that are important to us. This could be in regard to anything from what is true to us about our marriage to the way in which we want work done by our teams.

Leaders must create space for authentic communication to happen. Leo Buscaglia emphasizes how necessary this is:

> The need to create safe places where truth can be spoken and heard is one of the most important responsibilities of a hospitable leader.

"Communication, the art of talking with each other, saying what we feel and mean, saying it clearly, listening to what the other says and making sure that we're hearing accurately, is by all indication the skill most essential for creating and maintaining loving relationships." I can't imagine a more important leadership effort than ensuring that the people we lead feel at home enough to be who they really are, and feel safe enough to engage in honest interactions that promote love and spiritual growth.

I believe that we need to see ourselves as both host and guests in the business of hospitable communication. Sometimes we welcome strangers, sometimes we are the stranger, and sometimes both are true in the same setting. I think about this whenever I speak publicly. On one hand I am the host who is welcoming people into a communicative space I am creating. On the other hand, I am a guest, because the people I am speaking to are deciding whether or not they really want to hear and possibly respond to what I am saying or to just be in the same physical or technological space as I am while I speak. In order for my speaking to be effective, they must invite me in and welcome me and what I have to say. I must be a good guest.

Those of us who are Christ-followers live in this world amid the constant tension of host and stranger. We are in the world, and have responsibilities to care for it, while at the same time we are not of this world: "You must honor God while you live as strangers here on earth." Learning to live as guest and host is an essential skill, particularly in communication.

Three simple activities can help us create a hospitable communicative climate and effectively play our roles of hosts and guests: Accentuating areas of common grace. Listening. Speaking.

First, we must accentuate areas of common grace. Communication begins with finding things in common. Our English word *communication* comes from the Latin *communis*, which has to do with having something in common.

Knowing that communication is rooted in common bonds leads me to explore the space of common grace. Common grace was a prominent theme in the theology of Abraham Kuyper—a Dutch politician, journalist, statesman, and theologian who was prime minister of the Netherlands from 1901 to 1905. Kuyper made a distinction between the special grace that comes to those who believe in Jesus and "common grace as the universal bestowal by the Spirit of natural, moral and artistic gifts to believer and nonbeliever alike. Public and natural conscience, natural pity, some religious knowledge and a universal God-consciousness are parts of common grace." As human beings, what we have in common—different as we may be—is a larger part of our story than we often acknowledge.

We are all created in God's image. We all have a need to love and be loved. We all have an instinct to connect to the Transcendent. Regardless of our culture, we generally find commonality in what we consider to be beautiful—a sunset, for instance. And we each have a God-given awareness that there is a difference between right and wrong.

Hospitable communication begins with a desire to find things in common. Before we discuss what we don't agree on, we need to revel in the good and beautiful things we can appreciate and enjoy together. This could be art or athletics—a concern for the community or love for our children—common business goals, or a desire to make a positive difference in the world. Stoppe noted, "By His words and actions, Jesus observed a cardinal rule of effective communication: You persuade a person only to the extent that you come into his world of experience, speak his language, and identify your message with his needs, motives, and desires. . . . In a similar manner, we are always preconditioned by our needs, goals and desires."

I had a crazy experience a number of years ago that reminds me to accentuate areas of commonality even in matters specific to the family of faith—those who have received God's special grace. A new member of our staff team had planned her wedding in a Catholic church in the parish of her husband-to-be. Sharon and I accepted the invitation to attend in order to support this young couple on their big day. I found myself there a little early, sitting on the second row in the large cathedral. Frankly, I was relieved to not be the officiant for once and was catching up on some work on my phone, hoping the ceremony would begin soon and be over soon so I could get on with my day soon. I was jarred when someone tapped me on the shoulder and said, "Father Mike would like to see you in the sacristy." I said, "Okay. . . . What is a sacristy?"

As a Protestant I had virtually no personal experience with anything about Roman Catholicism even though a large percentage of my congregation was born and raised Roman Catholic. Anyway, I soon learned the sacristy was what I would call the pastor's office—or maybe the green room—except that this was also where the sacred vessels and vestments were kept.

Father Mike told me that he had received permission from the archdiocese to ask me to participate in the service and that it would really mean a lot to the bride and groom if I would read a passage from the Gospels. I politely demurred, "I'd much rather sit in the audience with my wife. I'm looking forward to watching you officiate the ceremony." Well, Father Mike—and now the groom—were quite persuasive. Not wanting to disappoint anyone, and hoping that we would just get the thing started, I finally said yes.

And then Father Mike added, "Would you mind also doing a short sermon? It would mean a lot to the bride and groom." Not from the main pulpit, he stressed, because I am not a Catholic priest, but from a secondary pulpit where a Catholic layman—or a Protestant pastor, I guess—could speak. I didn't know what to say. So I said yes. And then Father Mike opened the closet and started rummaging around in it and came out with a long white . . . robe? "You need to wear this," he said. Politely, I tried to decline: "I'm not comfortable wearing the clerical robes of a Catholic priest." "Well, if you are going to read the Gospel and do a sermon, you need to wear this robe," he said. "It would mean a lot to the bride and groom."

Suffice it to say that I ended up virtually co-officiating the service, including reading the Gospel, giving a spontaneous sermon, and joining in a lengthy back-and-forth intercessory prayer with Father Mike for the bride and groom and about nearly everyone and everything else on the entire planet. All while wearing the white robe of a Roman Catholic priest. And I had a ball. More important, the bride and groom were thrilled by this extemporaneous and joyful partnership between the bride's nondenominational pastor and the groom's Catholic priest.

As you are probably well aware, Roman Catholics and Protestants haven't had much to do with each other over the past five hundred years or so. There are significant and important disagreements about our understanding and practice of Christianity. But on that day I was reminded that we have a lot in common. We read from the same Gospel. We prayed to the same Lord. And together we led a young couple into the covenant—or sacrament—of marriage. So if I had to wear a robe over my perfectly appropriate black Italian suit and tie to enter into that world in that moment to be a good guest, in order to accomplish something good and beautiful, so be it. Here's what I know: Saying yes to Father Mike and being a good guest in that common space created the possibility of having conversations about things we disagree on—if that seems important to do—in the future. Hospitable communication accentuates what we have in common.

Second, for us to practice hospitable communication, we must focus on empathetic listening. Jesus said that we can listen but not hear. When we really listen we genuinely seek to understand another person. We want to comprehend their thoughts, feelings, experiences, and point of view. We want to see what they see, whether we agree with them or not.

We must listen to understand before we speak in order for what we speak to have a greater likelihood of being received.

> **If we are going to connect with our audience, we must be a good audience first.**

If we are going to connect with our audience, we must *be* a good audience first—before the conversation or speech or sermon. Robert McKee, the legendary screenwriting teacher and author of the breakthrough *Story: Substance, Structure, Style, and the Principles of Screenwriting*, wrote that when talented people write well it is usually because they are "moved by a desire to touch the audience." He talks about how smart an audience of filmgoers is and that "it's all a writer can do, using every bit of craft he's mastered, to keep ahead of the sharp perceptions of a focused audience. No film can be made to work without an understanding of the reactions and anticipations of the audience." I try to always keep in mind that my audience is smarter than I am.

The apostle Paul encouraged us to "be humble, thinking of others as better than yourselves." I believe this is an essential mindset for hospitable communication. I assume that before I can teach my audience, I need to learn from them. They know things—particularly about themselves—that I do not, and I must tap in to their knowledge if I am going to say something of value to them.

Eugene Peterson, in his marvelous autobiography *The Pastor*, tells us about a seminarian who asked an unusually gifted preacher, "What is the most important thing you can do to preach each Sunday?" To which the preacher replied, "For two hours every Tuesday and Thursday afternoon, I walk through the neighborhood and make home visits. There is no way that I can preach the Gospel to the people if I don't know how they are living or what they are thinking and talking about." If we work hard to listen to the people we are to speak to, we will know what to say—and how to say it most effectively. We must each find our own ways of gathering intelligence from our audience—whoever that audience may be.

I also listen *while* I speak. People are always communicating, even when they are not saying anything. I love that line in *A River Runs Through It* when the Presbyterian minister/fly fisherman/father sits reading on the riverbank while his sons fish in the rapidly flowing river. When one of them comes over to where he is sitting, he says, "If you listen carefully, you will hear that the words are underneath the water." Great communicators are able to hear what is not being said, especially while they are talking. I think any of us can learn to do this if we care enough about our audience to pay attention. To listen.

Third, we speak. And we do not only speak what our audience wants to hear. We love people too much for that. We speak what people need to hear. We speak truth as best as we understand it and as carefully as it can be said. If we have begun our communication effort with accentuating what we have in common, and if we have listened to understand, then we have presumably created space where truth can be spoken. Even then we never just rush in and hit someone over the head with it. We take care to find just the right moment to speak because "truth uttered prematurely is a serious liability."

And we take great care to choose our words and craft our message so that we speak truth hospitably. This is eloquently demonstrated in the story of how John Henry Jowett, a famous British preacher of another era, "was walking with a friend in a Birmingham park. His friend wanted to show him how the Holly Blue butterfly differed from the Common Blue. With the utmost caution he approached the resting insect so that he could lift it off the leaf without injury to show him the markings on the underside of the wings. Jowett watched in silence and then said, 'That is just how I pick a word.'"

As usual, the apostle Paul says this about as well as it can be said: "Be wise in the way you act toward outsiders; make the most of every opportunity. Let your conversation be always full of grace, seasoned with salt, so that you may know how to answer everyone." . . . or . . . "Talk to them agreeably and with a flavor of wit, and try to fit your answers to the needs of each one."

We speak kind words: "Worry can rob you of happiness, but kind words will cheer you up." We speak gentle words: "A gentle answer turns away wrath, but a harsh word stirs up anger." We speak gracious words: ". . . gracious words promote instruction." We speak honest words: "An honest answer is like a kiss on the lips." We speak wise words: "Thoughtless words can wound as deeply as any sword, but wisely spoken words can heal."

We must always remember that we are obligated to speak truth—to whoever it is in whatever leadership context—because we love people and want them to grow. "Better is open rebuke than hidden love." And we must also remember our obligation, as hospitable leaders, to speak lovingly. We speak the truth, and when we do we wrap it in grace. We speak the truth and hope that as we do, people feel home. That their hearts are warmed. And that they welcome us in.

Leadership Take-Homes

1. **Promote grace and truth.** Hospitable leaders do not shy away from truth but foster a love-infused communicative climate in which truth can be spoken and received.

2. **Hospitable communication places leaders in the role of both host and guest.** We are hosts when welcoming others into the communicative space, and we are guests when addressing individuals or groups.

3. **Accentuate areas of common grace.** To communicate hospitably, we must find commonalities and listen before, while, and after speaking.

Sources

"I propose that love": Rodney Ferris, "How Organizational Love Can Improve Leadership," *Organizational Dynamics*, Vol. 16. No. 4. doi.org /10.1016/0090-2616(88)90011-3.

Truth must be spoken.: Ephesians 4:15.

"full of grace": John 1:14.

The truth will set us free.: John 8:32.

"Jesus' inclusivity is not without expectations.": Elizabeth Newman, *Untamed Hospitality: Welcoming God and Other Strangers* (Grand Rapids: Brazos Press, 2007), 31.

"Let any one of you who": John 8:7.

"Go now and leave your life of sin.": John 8:11.

"You can't handle the truth!": *A Few Good Men*, directed by Rob Reiner, written by Aaron Sorkin, film (Columbia Pictures, 1992).

"To fail to confront when confrontation is required": M. Scott Peck, *The Road Less Traveled* (New York: Simon & Schuster, 1978), 106.

"love . . . rejoices": 1 Corinthians 13:6.

"Communicative climate": Richard L. Stoppe, *Leadership Communication: A Scriptural Perspective* (Cleveland: Pathway Press, 1982), 61.

"Communication, the art of talking": Leo Buscaglia, *Loving Each Other: The Challenge of Human Relationships* (Thorofare: SLACK, 1984), 53.

"You must honor God": 1 Peter 1:17 CEV.

Communication comes from the Latin *communis*: Webster's Dictionary.

"common grace as the universal": Jim Belcher, *Deep Church: A Third Way Beyond Emerging and Traditional* (Downers Grove: InterVarsity Press, 2009), 193.

"By his words and actions": Richard L. Stoppe, *Leadership Communication*, 15–16.

Jesus said that we can listen: Mark 8:18.

"moved by a desire to touch": Robert McKee, *Story: Substance, Structure, Style, and The Principles of Screenwriting* (New York: Harper Collins, 1997), 7–8.

"be humble, thinking of others": Philippians 2:3 NLT.

"What is the most important thing": Eugene H. Peterson, *The Pastor* (New York: Harper Collins, 2011), 86, 87.

"If you listen carefully": Norman Maclean, "A River Runs Through It," in *A River Runs Through It and Other Stories* (Chicago: University of Chicago Press, 1976), 109.

"truth uttered prematurely": Richard L. Stoppe, *Leadership Communication*, 21.

"was walking with a friend": Donald McCullough, *Say Please, Say Thank You* (New York: G. P. Putnam, 1998), 178.

"Be wise in": Colossians 4:5–6.

"Talk to them agreeably": Colossians 4:6 NJB.

"Worry can rob": Proverbs 12:25 GNT.

"A gentle answer": Proverbs 15:1.

"gracious words promote instruction": Proverbs 16:21.

"An honest answer": Proverbs 24:26.

"Thoughtless words can": Proverbs 12:18 GNT.

"Better is open": Proverbs 27:5.

9

People Are Opportunities

One of my pet peeves—and sadly I have several of them—is when someone uses the response "No problem" when the hospitable response would be "You're welcome," or some variation of "My pleasure." A simple example: I call an office and a receptionist answers the phone. I ask for someone and the receptionist says, "I'll transfer you." I say, "Thank you," to which the receptionist replies, "No problem." I think, *Problem? Who said anything about a problem? Could it possibly be a problem for you to perform this most difficult task? Am I potentially a problem? Do you feel like you may need to solve me or this trouble I have somehow stirred up?* I probably sound a little neurotic here, but I hope you get my point. The phrase "no problem" is off-limits for our team.

Visit a restaurant or hotel where employees are well trained in hospitality and see if they ever say "No problem." Nope. They say things like, "It is my pleasure to serve you," or, "You are so welcome. Is there anything else I can do?" Why? Because people are not problems. We ought not use the language of problem when we are dealing with people.

Many times a leader's effectiveness is dramatically stunted because we do not seem to understand that relating with other people—serving people, working with people—is always an opportunity. Always. Max De Pree rocked my world years ago when he wrote, "A leader first makes a personal commitment to be hospitable to gifted people." We must see people and the gifts they bring only through the lens of possibility. People are always our pleasure.

To be frank, I sometimes have to remind myself of what I just wrote. To always look at the people I am in relationship with—who I work with, who I work for—as my pleasure. I know that the grandest possibilities of life are found in relationship to others. I also know that my most formidable challenges are found in relationship with others. I often hear senior leaders say their greatest joy is leading the people on their teams, and their greatest struggle is leading the people on their teams.

We were made to need other people in every stage of life.

Regardless, as organizational behavior guru Margaret Wheatley wrote, "Relationships are all there is. Everything in the universe only exists because it is in relationship to everything else. Nothing exists in isolation. We have to stop pretending we are individuals who can go it alone." Scripture teaches that "none of us lives for ourselves alone, and none of us dies for ourselves alone." Both options seem bleak. We were made to need other people in every stage of life—even in dying. As Yogi Berra said, "Always go to other people's funerals, otherwise they won't go to yours." But I am not interested in discussing the dying part here. I want to stress the life and leadership part. We can only lead successfully if we learn to do it in synergistically healthy relationship to others.

Nothing in my work life has been more pleasurable than when I have successfully worked with others in a collaborative process. Systems scientist and MIT Senior Lecturer Peter Senge reminded us, "Most of us at one time or another have been part of a great team, a group of people who functioned together in an extraordinary way—who trusted one another, who complemented one another's strengths and compensated for one another's limitations, who had common goals that were larger than individual goals, and who produced extraordinary results. I have met many people who have experienced this sort of profound teamwork—in sports, or in the performing arts, or in business. Many say that they have spent much of their life looking for that experience again." We are wired to accomplish more when we work in unified effort with others, and we are wired to enjoy what we achieve more when we accomplish it with people we love.

We simply must find pleasure in creating collaborative teams. The instinct of great leaders to focus on people and harmonize their efforts to accomplish mission comes from God. We see this in the beginning when God created people in His image and tasked them to partner with Him in carrying out His mission. God did not need people—as we do—because He is completely happy and sufficient in himself. He created human beings because He wanted to do what was in His heart to do in the company of people. He invited people into the community of His three-in-one Self because He wanted to expand the team. He wanted people to join Him in His work. He found pleasure in people—and still does—even with all the challenges people bring.

The Boys in the Boat is a heartwarming story of how nine working-class boys from the Midwestern United States rowed to victory in eight-oar crew in the 1936 Berlin Olympics. These young men captured the attention of the world by dramatically defeating the German boat that rowed for Adolf Hitler. At the center of this historical tale is a teenager named Joe Ranz. Joe, impoverished and without family, was extremely talented yet had a difficult time learning to row in synchronization with the other boys in the boat. This independence became a threat to the success of his team.

His legendary coach, George Pocock, took Joe aside and told him that sometimes Joe seemed to think that he had to row the boat all by himself. He asserted that Joe had to learn to be thankful that there were other boys in the boat, and to care about them, open his heart to them, trust them. And then he inspired him with these words: "If you don't like some fellow in the boat, Joe, you have to learn to like him. It has to matter to you whether he wins the race, not just whether you do. . . . Joe, when you really start trusting those other boys, you will feel a power at work within you that is far beyond anything you've ever imagined. Sometimes, you will feel as if you have rowed right off the planet and are rowing among the stars."

I know that as a leader I cannot reach the potential of what I have been called to do if I am only focused on what I am doing. I must work just as hard—if not harder—to get other people in the boat, to communicate my care for them, and to organize our efforts so everyone wins as we accomplish our mission together. There are times when I am overwhelmed by the energy expended and complications inherent to any attempt to get people rowing in the same rhythms and direction. I have to remind myself that people are my pleasure, not my problems. I have to start with this mindset: I can't do it alone, and I don't want to do it alone. People are my pleasure. People are my pleasure. People are my pleasure.

If we are going to do meaningful things in the company of other people, we clearly must learn the art of hospitable communication. After all, as Stephen Covey posits, "Communication is the most important skill in life." My experience is that communicative abilities are almost always cited as the most critical factor in the success or failure of any relationship.

God himself created an incredibly hospitable communicative environment in the Garden of Eden, where He met regularly with His team to know and be known. I have to believe they talked about what they were doing together. This was the beginning of prayer—and prayer, if understood rightly, is perhaps the best example of the kind of communication necessary for a leader to build healthy teams. Prayer is communication between a person and God about who they are, and what they are thinking and doing together. We need to practice this kind of communication to most successfully work together with people.

Jesus modeled the communication efforts of a hospitable leader in a fascinating story recorded in the gospel of John. Simon Peter had been tasked by Jesus to play a lead role in the church, but had terribly failed by denying Him at the crucifixion. And Peter was dreadfully ashamed. John tells us that after the resurrection, Jesus appeared to His disciples on two occasions, but then appeared again to set up an interaction with Peter that resolved any lingering conflict and set out a vision for his future. Jesus did this when He invited Peter to breakfast. Actually, He *cooked* him breakfast.

Peter and the other disciples had been fishing all night on the Sea of Galilee. Early in the morning, when they came back to shore, Jesus was there. Peter, impulsive as usual, jumped out of the boat fully clothed and swam to shore. The other disciples followed in the boat. As Peter emerged from the water dripping wet, followed by his friends, Jesus was there waiting for them and "they saw a fire of burning coals there with fish on it, and some bread. . . . Jesus said to them, 'Come and have breakfast.'"

You have to love this picture of Jesus Christ cooking breakfast for His leadership team. The description of burning coals with fish and bread grilling over them, the sounds and smells drifting through the early morning salty mist, feels like an advertisement for a trendy Zagat-rated restaurant. But it's just the picture of an extremely hospitable leader providing a hospitable setting for an extremely important meeting.

When they finished eating, Jesus took Simon Peter for a walk on the shore of Galilee. He asked him challenging questions that Simon Peter answered in a way that signals the full restoration of their relationship. Jesus clarified Peter's leadership role. He charged him to follow Him and to fulfill his responsibilities regardless of the cost. And Peter reconnected to his destiny.

It is instructive to me that part of the leadership methodology Jesus practiced in this interaction with Peter was to ask him questions: "When they had finished eating, Jesus said to Simon Peter . . . 'Do you love me' . . . ?" From Eden forward it seems to me that God creates hospitable communicative environments where He engages in dialogue with members of His team. He asks lots of questions. In Eden He asked questions like, "Where are you?" "Who told you?" "What is this you have done?" It isn't as if God doesn't know the answers, but He wants the people He is leading to engage, to think, to feel, to will, to participate. You get the sense that He is all about what we are doing *together*.

Jesus is constantly showing us what God is like. As part of this, He often asks questions. In the gospel records Jesus asked an astonishing 307 questions. I know that folks say Jesus is the answer. And I agree. But He appears to have wanted people to work their way to the answer. This is central to effective collaboration. A leader does not dictate answers, but rather creates an environment where people can work together toward answers. We should consistently be asking people on our teams, "What do you think? What do you feel about this? What are you doing? What do you want to do? Can we make this thing happen together?"

It is no wonder we hear more and more about the power of collaborative leadership. I thoroughly enjoyed reading a unique take on collaborative creativity in Kelly Leonard and Tom Yorton's book *Yes, And*. They discussed the success of the Second City—a comedy enterprise well-known as the first ongoing improvisational comedy troupe. The Second City is particularly famous for its stable of actors, comedians, and directors, and has launched many celebrated talents into show business.

In *Yes, And* we are told that many of the lessons from improvisation can be applied to leadership in any organization, especially creativity, collaboration, and communication.

> We should consistently be asking people on our teams, "What do you think? ... Can we make this thing happen together?"

Two points from *Yes, And* strike me in the context of this chapter. First is the Second City's emphasis on ensembles: "We celebrate the stars who break out at the Second City, but they didn't become stars by working as solo acts; they did it by learning to work in groups. The ensemble is the preeminent focus of everything in our business, and it pops up everywhere— in sales teams, executive boards, retail staff—and it is a vital ingredient in almost any organization's growth and competitiveness." Second is the emphasis on co-creation: "Half a century of doing this work has shown us that dialogues push stories further than monologues. Our ensembles create art not only in front of the audience, but also in tacit conversation with the audience—seeking suggestions, monitoring feedback, and transforming material in turn. The sum of co-creation is greater than its parts."

I have been thinking a lot in recent years about a leadership activity relating to teams or ensembles, and co-creation that I believe is core to hospitable leadership and communication. I call it "pre-inspiration." Clearly one of the central activities a leader must engage in is inspiration, casting vision for a preferred future and asking people to join him or her in actual-izing it. What I have learned is that it is much easier to inspire people to a future they have participated in envisioning and are co-creating. When I was much younger, I misguidedly thought that effective leaders walked into a meeting with people they hoped to inspire, with an already fully developed plan to inspire them to implement. I have since learned that I do not want to develop a plan without stakeholder involvement at the very least. I want to collaborate with my ensemble to craft vision, to figure out how to articulate our mission, and to develop strategies. I want us to co-create the future.

When we began to master design a new Worship and Mis-sion Center for The Life Christian Church many years ago, we involved a representative group of members on several teams who worked together to inform the design. Within the pa-rameters of our already agreed-upon mission, each team was charged with the responsibility of making recommendations to our lead team and architect as to how some part of the building might best facilitate what we believe we are called to do. So, of course, people involved in our children's ministry spoke into the design of our children's ministry space while worship-arts people informed the design of the stage and wor-ship technologies. And so on. Not rocket science, I know. But here is part of what I learned in that simple process: When it was time to inspire people to give sacrificially to actually build that building, it was a lot easier to inspire them to give to something they had helped create.

Leadership is not—as still too many people intimate—getting people to do something the leader believes they should do and then making them think that they thought of it. That is not hospitable leadership. That is manipulation. A hospitable leader inspires people to do things that they have already collaborated together on—that they did think of, or at least have thought about and have had impact—and that they have helped decide to do. They engage people at the level of creation, at the level of their will, as God does and has always done.

Often now I force myself to not come up with a finalized plan for something I think might be the right thing for us to do. Instead, I will walk into a meeting with stakeholders—board and elders, or my executive team, or creative team, or whatever team has a stake in what I want to lead us to create together—and I will say something like, "Here's something that I have been praying about . . . thinking about . . . that I believe could be possible . . . that we could do together." And I will stimulate discussion that I hope might lead us to create together that something, or something better than that something. I love creating great things in relationship with others. Even though working with people in this way is typically more complicated, it is exceedingly more effective and rewarding for everyone involved.

Leading groups of people to work together in co-creation demands a certain mastery of what is commonly called a democratic leadership communication style. As described in the text *Leadership: A Communication Perspective*, "The leader adopting the democratic communication style encourages follower involvement and participation in the determination of goals and procedures. Democratic leaders assume that followers are capable of making informed decisions. The democratic leader does not feel intimidated by the suggestions provided by followers but believes that the contributions of others improve the overall quality of decision making." I think it is fair to say that a democratic leadership style is more complicated than the two on either extreme—an authoritarian leadership communication style or a laissez-faire approach. But it is far more hospitable to people and more effective in the long term, particularly if a leader is interested at all in the self-actualization of followers as well as the accomplishment of organizational mission.

An authoritarian leader will just tell people what to do. There is not much leadership sophistication needed to do that. The research shows, however, that while an authoritarian leadership communication style can increase productivity—especially if a leader is present and watching—it kills creativity, promotes a just-beneath-the-surface disunity, and denies people the satisfaction and self-efficacy that comes through co-creation.

On the other extreme, a laissez-faire—or hands-off—leadership communication style, where little guidance is provided, decreases innovation and motivation and increases feelings of isolation and dissatisfaction among team members. This results in poor overall team performance. People need to be led—want to be led—by leaders who inspire them to work together to accomplish things that they are helping to create together. This is why, according to authors Craig Johnson and Michael Hackman, "Democratic leadership communication contributes to relatively high productivity (whether or not the leader directly supervises followers) and to increased satisfaction, commitment and cohesiveness. This style of communication is best suited for tasks that require participation and involvement, creativity, and commitment to a decision." This is the kind of communicative environment that is hospitable to people and their gifts. It necessitates a delicate leadership dance. We are leading, but in partnership with others. I find great joy in this.

I suggest that this dimension of hospitable leadership begins when we let people know how much we need them. But even more than need, we must convey want. We should constantly communicate that working collaboratively is not a problematic necessity or a complication, but our pleasure. We must express that we enjoy doing what we have been called to do so much more when we are doing it in concert with people we love.

Marshall Goldsmith observed, "When you declare your dependence on others they usually agree to help," and wrote that his wealth of experience with leaders has convinced him, "If you put all your cards in someone else's hands, that person will treat you better than if you kept the cards to yourself." That's been my experience as well.

One of the most gratifying involvements of my life has been my relationship with the board at The Life Christian Church: the people who—along with our elders—I both lead and collectively submit to. We have a rotating board; the longest any one person can serve in one stint is three years. That means that in more than two and half decades, a broad diversity of extremely capable men and women have served. Now—and if I believed in knocking on wood, I would knock on it now— we have never had a vote on our board in all the years of our existence that wasn't unanimous. This unanimity was never a goal. Somehow it has just happened. We have faced incredible challenges together, experienced great victories, and suffered our share of grief and setbacks. But we have always done it together. We have disagreed, debated, laughed uproariously, cried, decided, and decided not to decide, and all the other things people do when they are collaborating with others to move a mission forward. And we have always done it together. We have created our future together and are creating our future together.

People need to be led—want to be led—by leaders who inspire them to work together to accomplish things that they are helping to create together.

It seems to surprise people when I say this, but I love board meetings. I love leading in partnership with gifted people. And they do want me to lead. But I remind them often that I can't do this alone. I don't want to do it alone.

When people know that you need them in order to be successful, that you need them and the gifts they bring—their ideas, their candor, their partnership, their support—wonderful things happen. One more time: People are not problems; people are my pleasure.

Leadership Take-Homes

1. **People are our pleasure, not our problem.** Hospitable leaders see people and the gifts they bring through the lens of possibility.

2. **Collaboration is more rewarding than isolation.** We are wired to achieve more, and to enjoy achievement more, in unified effort with others.

3. **Hospitable leaders lean into their dependence on those they lead.** When we practice the "democratic communication style," we are more likely to both accomplish the mission and witness the self-actualization of those we lead.

Sources

"A leader first makes a personal commitment": Max De Pree, *Leadership Jazz: The Essential Elements of a Great Leader* (New York: Dell Publishing, 1992), 96.

"relationships are all there is.": Margaret Wheatley, *Turning to One Another: Simple Conversations to Restore Hope to the Future,* expanded edition (San Francisco: Berrett-Koehler Publishers, 2009), 23.

"none of us lives for ourselves": Romans 14:7.

"Always go to other people's funerals": Yogi Berra, *When You Come to a Fork in the Road, Take it! Inspiration and Wisdom from One of Baseball's Greatest Heroes* (New York: Hachette, 2002), 163.

"Most of us at one time or another": Peter Senge, *The Fifth Discipline: The Art and Practice of the Learning Organization* (New York: Doubleday, 1994), 4.

God created people in His image: Genesis 1:26–31.

"If you don't like some fellow": Daniel James Brown, *The Boys in the Boat* (New York: Penguin, 2013), 235.

"Communication is the most important skill in life.": Stephen Covey, *7 Habits of Highly Effective People* (New York: Simon & Schuster, 1989), 237.

Prayer is communication between a person and God: Richard J. Foster, et al. *The Renovaré Spiritual Formation Bible* (New York: Harper Collins, 2005), 1.

"they saw a fire": John 21:9, 12.

"When they had finished eating": John 21:15.

"Where are you?": Genesis 3:9.

"Who told you?": Genesis 3:11.

"What is this you have done?": Genesis 3:13.

"We celebrate the stars who break out": Kelly Leonard and Tom Yorton, *Yes, And: How Improvisation Reverses "No, But" Thinking and Improves Creativity and Collaboration—Lessons from The Second City* (New York: Harper Collins, 2015), 13–14.

"The leader adopting the Democratic": Craig E. Johnson and Michael Z. Hackman, *Leadership: A Communication Perspective* (Long Grove: Waveland Press, 2004), 38, 42.

authoritarian leader . . . laissez-faire: Johnson and Hackman, 42.

"Democratic leadership communication contributes": Johnson and Hackman, 44.

"When you declare your dependence": Marshall Goldsmith, *What Got You Here Won't Get You There* (New York: Hachette, 2011), 86.

10

Communication Champion

L eaders must be communication champions. Regardless
of what we are leading, we must see ourselves as the person accountable for ensuring that there is a hospitable
communicative climate. We are the responsible party.

It is important not to confuse a democratic communication
style—which I advocated in the previous chapter—with the
abdication of ultimate leadership responsibility. Every organization needs a leader—or in some cases leaders—charged
with setting the overall direction of the organization and making sure the environmental conditions enable success.

Even the most collaborative communicative environments
need a leader who sets the course and the tone for the organization. Warren Bennis and Patricia Biederman wrote a riv-
eting book about the secrets of creative collaboration. They
studied a number of great groups that have reshaped the world
in significant ways. They emphasize that in all but the rarest
of cases, a singular person does not produce greatness. "The
leader finds greatness in the group." Yet even then they stress
great groups "all have extraordinary leaders . . . virtually every

great group has a strong and visionary head." It is paradoxical. We are called to lead people in a way that involves them meaningfully in working together with us, and one another, in creating a preferred future. But we are still called to lead. We are the responsible party.

If the environment—of our family, team, business, classroom, nonprofit, or church—is not a grace-filled place where hospitable communication is occurring at every level, we are the responsible party. If a compelling vision and mission is not constantly articulated and responded to, we are the responsible party. If organizational values are unclear and not being lived out, we are the responsible party. If there are communication silos where one person or team or department is not sharing critical information with others, we are the responsible party.

Communication can technically be understood as the sending and receiving of signals. Many people seem to believe that they have communicated when they have sent a signal. They told someone something—or sent a memo, or left a message, or made a speech, or nodded their head. But that does not mean we have communicated. We have not communicated unless we get a signal back that lets us know that our message was received and understood. A communicator encodes a message (or figures out how to say something to someone) and sends it through whatever channel is appropriate to his or her intended audience, or receiver. Hopefully then, the receiver decodes the message (or tries to figure out exactly what the sender has said) and sends back some response that lets the communicator know that they have been accurately heard. Only when we are satisfied that what we meant to say has been received and understood can we know that we have communicated.

I write this for three reasons: First, the leader must be a good signal sender *and* receiver. Second, as communication champions, we must insist that signal-sending and signal-receiving is happening throughout and from whatever we are leading. I frequently ask myself and my team, "How do we know that what we are trying to say is actually being received?" And I remind us that in both our interpersonal and organizational communication efforts, we have not been successful unless we know we have been accurately heard, and that we only know we have been accurately heard when we hear back.

Third, I know that I must create an environment where people feel comfortable sending signals back. I want to make sure people feel enough at home with me and in the environment of the organization that they know it's safe to be who they really are and truly say what they think and feel. As a hospitable leader, I must accept responsibility to foster a communicative atmosphere where people feel at home enough to authentically communicate with me and one another.

There is a great verse in Ephesians that demonstrates an extraordinarily crucial principle: "I pray that Christ will be more and more at home in your hearts, living within you as you trust in him." The capacity for someone to be more and more at home with us increases as trust increases. Even Jesus. And it goes both ways: In this passage, Jesus can only be more and more at home as we trust Him. In another passage, He could not be at home with people because He did not trust them: "Many people saw the signs he was performing and believed . . . but Jesus would not entrust himself to them, for he knew all people. . . . He knew what was in each person."

Trust is a wonderful word to use to talk about producing the conditions in which people are at home and can share who they really are. Dr. Henry Cloud wrote that "to trust means to be careless. It means that you do not have to worry about how to 'take care' of yourself with that person, because he is going to be worried about that too. It means that you do not have to 'guard' yourself with her, because she is going to be concerned with what is good for you and what is not good for you. You do not have to 'watch your back' with him, because he is going to be watching it for you."

Imagine being so at home with the people on your team that you can talk about your hopes and dreams and concerns and challenges knowing that everyone there is for you and your success. Imagine being able to openly acknowledge and apologize for a mistake knowing that you will be treated graciously. Imagine being able to talk to someone honestly and constructively about their poor job performance knowing that they will be grateful. And imagine the people on your team feeling safe enough to be who they really are and share what they truly think and feel with you, knowing that they will be received with love and respect.

Stephen M. R. Covey, in his book *The Speed of Trust*, celebrates the benefits of engendering high-trust environments where people and organizations can flourish. Based on extensive research and feedback, he asserts that in high-trust organizational environments,

Information is shared openly.

Mistakes are tolerated and encouraged as a way of learning.

The culture is innovative and creative.

People are loyal to those who are absent.

People talk straight and confront real issues.

There is real communication and real collaboration.

People share credit abundantly.

There are few "meetings after the meetings."

Transparency is a practiced value.

People are candid and authentic.

There is a high degree of accountability.

There is palpable vitality and energy.

People can feel the positive momentum.

When I read Covey's words I think, *I'd love to work in a place like that.* And then I remind myself that I am a leader. I can create a place like that. I must accept responsibility to constantly upgrade the climate in my spheres of influence from low trust to high trust.

In order to create a high-trust environment where people feel more and more at home, I think the leader needs to be more and more at home. We can extend trust to others by taking the risk to be who we really are. This demands a certain level of vulnerability. A leader who is strong enough to be appropriately vulnerable is sending a signal to his or her followers that he or she trusts them enough to be their authentic self. When people feel trusted, they become more inclined to trust the leader back.

Patrick Lencioni calls this "getting naked." He writes, in his book of the same name aimed at management consultants, "Without the willingness to be vulnerable, we will not build deep and lasting relationships in life. That's because there is no better way to earn a person's trust than by putting ourselves in a position of unprotected weakness and demonstrating that we believe they will support us." In a world where we have been taught that a leader is a never-see-me-sweat, I-have-all-the-answers, I-do-not-acknowledge-weakness-or-make-mistakes person, this soul nakedness is not easy. Not for me, anyway. But I know that I do sweat, that I don't have all the answers, that I

> A leader who is strong enough to be appropriately vulnerable is sending a signal to his or her followers that he or she trusts them enough to be their authentic self.

do have glaring weaknesses, and do make mistakes. So who am I kidding? I might as well be who I really am with the people I am trying to lead. And as I learn to trust them more with who I am, I hope they learn to trust me more with who they are.

Vulnerability implies that we are capable of being wounded. There are times when I have extended trust to a person or people in what I later learned was a low-trust environment. Frankly, I regretted letting them see who I really am. We all need boundaries that protect our hearts from those who might wantonly wound us—and there are certainly people like that. But on the whole, the more trust I have extended, the more I find myself surrounded with people who love me for who I am. This is a wonderful experience for a leader.

So we need to extend trust and then we must prove trustworthy. The people around us need to know that if they are willing to be vulnerable—to trust us with who they are—they will not be hurt or disappointed. They need to know they can really be at home with us.

One of our staff team values at The Life Christian Church is "Reciprocal Candor." I instinctively tend to say what I truly think and feel. My problem has been learning to say it hospitably. I learned, however, that the people around me often did not feel at home enough with me to say what they truly thought or felt. That's not all that unusual, I guess. A study in *Well Being* intimates that most people would rather have a root canal than have a one-on-one meeting with their boss. But I don't want to be that kind of boss.

Slowly but surely, we have made Reciprocal Candor part of our culture. This means that we encourage and expect leaders to be honest with their team members, and team members to be just as honest back. We are still working hard to make sure people feel progressively more comfortable practicing this. I desperately want the people I'm working with to know that they can trust me enough to be completely candid with me. That they owe it to the other members of the team to be candid with them as well. And that when they speak the truth in love they will be rewarded for it—not exiled to the outer parts of the earth.

Another way to get at this is to challenge ourselves to foster an atmosphere of "psychological safety." Psychological safety is a culture within groups that Amy Edmondson, Harvard Business School professor, defines as a "shared belief held by members of a team that the team is safe for interpersonal risk-taking . . . a sense of confidence that the team will not embarrass, reject or punish someone for speaking up." Psychological safety "describes a team climate characterized by interpersonal trust and mutual respect in which people are comfortable being themselves." The leader is responsible for creating a hospitable communicative environment. We simply must accept this charge.

The tragic story of King David and his rebellious son Absalom—which took place some one thousand years before Christ—offers a powerful illustration of the inordinate power a leader has to determine environmental conditions. The name Absalom is often spoken in derision because of the insurrection he led against his father and king. The seed of this uprising, however, is not often exposed, but when it is, it is easy to see that David was at least as responsible for creating the conditions in which rebellion could blossom as Absalom was for his infamous treason.

Here's how it all began: "In the course of time, Amnon son of David fell in love with Tamar, the beautiful sister of Absalom son of David. . . . and since he was stronger than she, he raped her. . . . Her brother Absalom said to her, 'Has that Amnon, your brother, been with you? Be quiet for now, my sister; he is your brother. Don't take this thing to heart.' And Tamar lived in her brother Absalom's house, a desolate woman. When King David heard all this, he was furious."

David may have been furious, but he did not confront or punish Amnon. Two years later Absalom took matters into his own hands and killed the brother who had abused his sister. Then Absalom fled to a place called Geshur, far away from where his family—and his king—lived in Jerusalem. He stayed there, banished from his father's presence, for three years.

Scripture tells us that Joab, David's general and confidant, "knew that the king's heart longed for Absalom." So he arranged for a woman known for her wisdom to deliver an inspired message to David. She challenged him: "The king has not brought back his banished son . . . but that is not what God desires; rather, he devises ways so that a banished person does not remain banished from him." Convicted, David told Joab to bring Absalom back: "The king said . . . 'go, bring back the young man Absalom . . . but . . . he must go to his own house; he must not see my face.'"

Absalom lived in Jerusalem for two years without seeing his father. Twice he tried to convince Joab to arrange a reunion with the king. Joab refused. And then, in desperation, Absalom set Joab's barley fields on fire. This got Joab's attention. When he confronted Absalom, he learned his true motivation. Absalom just wanted to see his father and he acted out in a way that forced the issue.

> Absalom said to Joab, "Look, I sent word to you and said, 'Come here so I can send you to the king to ask, "Why have I come from Geshur? It would be better for me if I were still there!"' Now then, I want to see the king's face, and if I am guilty of anything, let him put me to death." So Joab went to the king and told him this. Then the king summoned Absalom, and he came in and bowed down with his face to the ground before the king. And the king kissed Absalom.

Tragically, by the time David finally kissed Absalom, it was too late. Nine years of rejection and separation had engendered an environment where bitterness grew into all-out rebellion. Absalom stole the hearts of the people of Israel and, four years after what had appeared to be a reconciliation with David, led an insurrection. Now David had to flee Jerusalem.

During the civil war that followed, David received word that Absalom had been killed. Though the rebellion was thwarted and the kingdom reunited, David was inconsolable. "The king was shaken . . . and wept . . . 'O my son Absalom! My son, my son Absalom! If only I had died instead of you—O Absalom, my son, my son!'"

I feel like crying every time I read this. David did not need to have died for his son, he just needed to have kissed him sooner. Though Absalom was fully accountable for his own actions, I can't help but read this story and wonder what would have happened if David had led differently during all those years preceding the climax of this tragedy.

Absalom's name, by the way, is a combination of two relatively familiar Hebrew words—even in the English language: *abba* and *shalom*. Absalom means *father of peace* or *peace with the father*. One could read this story and easily concede that for many years, all Absalom really wanted was peace with his father. Until he didn't.

Shalom is an instructive word and concept. Shalom is more than just peace as we often think of it—the absence of conflict. Shalom is the condition of everything working harmoniously together the way everything is supposed to work. Shalom describes things as they were meant to be. Leaders have disproportionate power—and the obligation—to cause the condition of shalom.

Isaiah the prophet said that when Jesus came, shalom would increase as His influence increased. "Of the increase of his government and peace [shalom] there shall be no end." I think this is one of the ways we know if we are leading well. As our sphere of influence increases, environmental conditions should be changing from the way things ought not to be to the way things should be. There should be an increase of shalom under our leadership.

I have observed an Absalom dynamic in organizations—and families—in ways great and small over the years: the thing that didn't get dealt with when it should have festers, and a seed of bitterness produces poisonous fruit. A reconcilable relationship issue becomes an irreconcilable difference. A temporary separation turns into a banishment. Someone doesn't get the attention they need and they burn down a field. The kiss comes too late. Something that once was full of possibility becomes a tragedy. Instead of shalom, things are not the way they should be. And a place that is supposed to be home, where people and dreams flourish, becomes a place where a leader's heart is broken.

> As our sphere of influence increases, environmental conditions should be changing from the way things ought not to be to the way things should be.

In the distant past, when these kinds of things happened in my leadership setting, I would try to find someone to blame. Now I blame myself. Whoever did whatever they did is accountable for their own actions. But I am the leader and I am accountable for the overall climate where I lead.

I must practice an extreme ownership. I am moved by the work of retired Navy SEAL officers and now management consultants Jocko Willink and Leif Babin: "On any team, in any organization, all responsibility for success and failure rests with the leader. The leader must own everything in his or her world. There is no one else to blame. The leader must acknowledge mistakes and admit failures, take ownership of them, and develop a plan to win." As leaders or parents—especially parents—the atmosphere of the organization or family is on us. We must own this.

I do not mean to say that if we are good leaders we will not have to deal with people who stir up yucky stuff through no direct fault of ours. Remember that one-twelfth of Jesus' leadership team was named Judas. Remember that even though God created the most hospitable environment one can conceive of in Eden, people still made the choice to rebel. But the wise woman who finally convinced David to bring Absalom back home was exactly right when she told him that God "devises ways so that a banished person does not remain banished from him." God practiced extreme ownership for all of broken humanity. He accepted responsibility for sins He did not commit. He devised a way, through the work of Jesus, to bring His banished sons and daughters back home. That's what leaders do. We devise ways. We accept responsibility to create environments where people can be at home.

Leadership Take-Homes

1. **The hospitable leader works to become a communication champion.** We must be adept at sending and receiving signals.

2. **To achieve a high-trust environment, leaders must be strong enough to be appropriately vulnerable.** We need to extend trust to those we lead, then prove ourselves trustworthy. No one—not even Jesus—is at home with people they do not trust.

3. **Hospitable leaders create the conditions for shalom.** We must practice extreme ownership and accept responsibility for the overall climate of our leadership domain.

Sources

Leaders must be communication champions: Richard Daft, *The Leadership Experience,* 2nd edition (Mason: Thomson, 2002), 318.

"The leader finds greatness": Warren Bennis and Patricia Biederman, *Organizing Genius: The Secrets of Creative Collaboration* (Reading: Perseus, 1997), 3, 12.

Communication can be understood: Richard Daft, *The Leadership Experience,* 317.

"I pray that Christ": Ephesians 3:17 TLB.

"Many people saw": John 2:23–25.

"to trust means to be": Dr. Henry Cloud, *Integrity: The Courage to Meet the Demands of Reality* (New York: Harper Collins, 2006), 77.

"Information is shared openly": Stephen M. R. Covey, *The Speed of Trust: The One Thing that Changes Everything* (New York: Free Press, 2006), 237.

"Without the willingness to be": Patrick Lencioni, *Getting Naked: A Business Fable about Shedding the Three Fears that Sabotage Client Loyalty* (San Francisco: Jossey-Bass, 2010), vii.

Most people would rather have a root canal than have a one-on-one meeting: Tom Rath and Jim Harter, *Well Being: The Five Essential Elements* (New York: Gallup Press, 2010), 25.

"shared belief . . . describes a team": Charles Duhigg, "What Google Learned From Its Quest to Build the Perfect Team," *The New York Times Magazine,* February 25, 2016, https://www.nytimes.com/2016/02/28/magazine/what-google-learned-from-its-quest-to-build-the-perfect-team.html.

"In the course of time": 2 Samuel 13:1.

"and since he was": 2 Samuel 13:14.

"Her brother Absalom said to her": 2 Samuel 13:20–21.

"knew that the king's heart": 2 Samuel 14:1.

"The king has not brought back": 2 Samuel 14:13–14.

"The king said": 2 Samuel 14:21, 24.

"Absalom said to Joab": 2 Samuel 14:32–33.

"The king was shaken": 2 Samuel 18:33.

"Of the increase of his": Isaiah 9:7 KJV.

Shalom is more than just peace as we often think of it: Cornelius Plantinga Jr., *Not the Way It's Supposed to Be* (Grand Rapids: William B. Eerdmans Publishing, 1995).

"On any team, in any organization": Jocko Willink and Leif Babin, *Extreme Ownership: How US Navy SEALs Lead and Win* (New York: St. Martin's Press, 2015), 30.

"devises ways so that": 2 Samuel 14:14.

11

The Usefulness of Beautiful Things

Matthew tells an enchanting story in his gospel about something beautiful that happened to Jesus just a few days before His death. He was enjoying an unhurried dinner in the company of His friends, reclining at the table as was the custom, when a woman came to Him with an elegant bottle of very expensive perfume and lovingly poured it on His head—an act of extravagant worship. Instead of being impressed by the reverent generosity of this woman, Jesus' disciples were indignant. They said the costly perfume had been wasted on Jesus, that it could have been sold at a high price and the money given to the poor. Aware of their negative response to this gesture, Jesus said to them, "Why are you bothering this woman? She has done a beautiful thing to me. The poor you will always have with you, but you will not always have me." He told them that this perfume had been poured on His body to physically demonstrate what He had been trying to tell them about His imminent death and burial, and that this woman's act would be used to help tell His story all over the world.

I'm struck by the fact that Jesus celebrated the woman for doing this lavishly beautiful thing—pouring expensive perfume on His head—rather than what would have appeared to be the most useful thing—giving money to the poor. Clearly He cared deeply about the poor, and throughout His ministry repeatedly emphasized our responsibility to take care of those in need, but in this case He counted this extravagant act as a good deed. Some translations of this passage render "she has done a beautiful thing" as "She has done a good work," or "She has done a good deed." The word translated "good" or "beautiful" here intimates that what is beautiful is good. And from this story, we also get a hint that beauty can prove useful—especially in telling God's story. It occurs to me that there are times when doing a beautiful thing—even an extravagant and expensive beautiful thing—is the best way to do a good and useful thing.

Beauty is integral to hospitable communicative environments.

I want to make a case for investing in beautiful things. Beauty is integral to hospitable communicative environments. Beauty creates a climate that opens people's hearts to more than what can be physically sensed. Abraham Heschel said that beautiful art, for instance, "introduces us to emotions which we have never cherished before. . . . Great works produce rather than satisfy needs by giving the world fresh cravings." Beauty causes us to wonder. It points us to God and good.

Some of the greatest minds in history make the point that we are more receptive to what can be communicated about God in the presence of the beautiful. French physicist and theologian Pascal said that "every man is almost always led to believe not through proof, but through that which is attractive." C.S. Lewis explained part of his journey to faith as a longing "to find the place where all the beauty came from." An environment infused with beauty is an environment where people are more likely to pay attention to whatever is being communicated. I think this is not only true regarding God but anything true and good. We can invest in beauty in any leadership context knowing that the people we are leading are more receptive to our efforts to influence them in an appealing setting.

Our hearts are warmed by beauty and, as I mentioned earlier, when our hearts are warm, we can really listen. We really listen with our hearts. In the Greek language, the word *beautiful* is not only associated with the idea of good but also "includes the notion of 'call.'" Beauty calls us to something more than what we can understand with corporeal perception. Something beyond the here and now. John O'Donohue teaches us that "the heart is the place where beauty arrives. . . . It was fashioned for an eternal kinship with beauty; God knew that the heart would always be wedded to him in desire; for the other name of God is beauty."

I submit that when we grasp the power of beauty, we will spare no possible effort or cost to do beautiful things. When we feature created beauty, or create beauty ourselves, we are practicing a hospitality rooted in God himself and generating an environment where things of importance can be conveyed in ways infinitely useful. Hospitable leaders are not primarily utilitarian. We are not use-the-quickest-most-efficient-least-expensive-way-to-get-it-done-and-it-doesn't-matter-what-it-looks-sounds-feels-tastes-or-smells-like kind of people. We expend the time and energy and make the necessary sacrifices to do beautiful things.

First, we do beautiful things because beauty is good in and of itself. Or we might say it is transcendently useful. I was irresistibly impacted years ago when I read a wonderful book called *Angels in the Architecture*. Douglas Jones and Douglas Wilson convicted me when they suggested that the utilitarian ugliness of so much that Christians do would cause one to conclude that we have forgotten the holiness of God. If "we would understand how beautiful His holiness is . . . we could not be kept from writing concertos and building cathedrals. . . . We were created to make beautiful things—in music, in stone, on canvas, and sculpted gardens, and in wonderful buildings." As I read this, I hear the words of Augustine ringing in my ears, "Too late came I to love thee, O thou Beauty both so ancient and so fresh." And I hear the psalmist pray, "Let the beauty of the Lord our God be upon us."

There is this interminable discussion as to whether it is even moral to invest in things that are not immediately pragmatic. My response to this is that beauty is not always practical, but it is always useful. It is useful because it reflects God's glory. It is useful because it honors God. It is useful because it moves people's hearts toward the transcendent. If beauty accomplishes nothing more than this, it is still useful.

I heard my son Christian having a conversation with another leader about programming Sunday worship. Christian mentioned a certain song our team performed that might not typically be used in a worship set. The leader asked, understandably, "But could the congregation sing it?" And Christian replied, "Probably not. But it was beautiful. It glorified God. The people were moved by it. And sometimes we just do beautiful things because they are beautiful." I propose that we must start from a premise that acknowledges that we should want to create an environment that is beautiful in every way just because we should—because it's the right thing to do.

Second, beauty can be practically useful. The woman who lavished Jesus with expensive perfume from an elegant bottle did a transcendently useful thing because it was beautiful. But it was also practically useful because it communicated something more about the impending death of Jesus than words alone could transmit. And it was practically useful because this act

of veneration is still being used two thousand years after it occurred to communicate part of the story of Jesus.

Beauty is good in and of itself because it points us to the
transcendent, but it can also be practical because it helps us
accomplish important work in the here and now.

Most of us are stewards of limited resources and must make
decisions about how much to allocate for aesthetic beauty
and how much to give to those in need. I think that as often
as possible we should approach this choice with a both-and
mindset rather than an either-or dichotomy. A major emphasis
of the ministry I lead are our Life Local
and Global Missions programs that serve
people in need in a plethora of ways both
locally and globally. As I write this chapter, our congregation was recognized
this week by the national YMCA for our
long-standing good work with the New-
ark YMCA's 260-bed homeless facility.
We have invested significant human and
financial resources over many years in
our effort to mentor homeless children,
provide clothing, remodel rooms, throw
huge monthly birthday celebrations and
an annual Christmas extravaganza, help
families transition from the Y to perma-
nent housing, and more. We are so grateful to be able to serve
others in this and similar missional efforts.

> **Beauty . . . points us to the transcendent, but it can also be practical because it helps us accomplish important work in the here and now.**

One reason we are able to do these kinds of good deeds is
because we have also invested in aesthetically beautiful things.
Over the years I have encouraged our community that if we give
to create beauty—performing arts and fine arts; fountains and
fireplaces; and furniture, buildings, and landscaped grounds—
we can cultivate a climate in which more people's hearts are
more open to the story about Jesus that we have to share. And

more people will join us—and even offer their money—in our mission to the poor in body and spirit. Beauty is transcendently useful and it is practically useful. One might even argue that there is little difference between the two.

I gently challenge each of us leading in any context: Do beautiful things. I like the approach of BMW's Chris Bangel, who said, "We don't make 'automobiles.' [We make] moving works of art that express the driver's love of quality." Each of us should think about more than just how to get people from here to there; we should think about how to do it beautifully.

Most of us can decide and act in ways that celebrate beauty. The literature teacher or art teacher has an easy job of this. But somehow the mathematics teacher must engender an environment where equations and formulas are conveyed in a style that speaks to the beauty of an ordered world. I assert that we all can find a way to make our work beautiful—the plumber, the trainer, and the cupcake maker. Beauty is good.

Former New York Governor Mario Cuomo, a prolific orator, famously said that a politician should campaign in poetry but govern in prose. I get his point, but I don't think I agree. Sometimes prose—just saying a thing plainly—fails to capture people's imaginations and open the heart to something more. "About the great events of life prose seems an inadequate means of expression," James Sire wrote. To communicate—even to ourselves—about love, death, victory, defeat, things that matter, we search for words capable of engaging the heart. Hospitable communicators embrace this challenge. We do not just attempt to say a thing; we work hard to say it artfully. Beautifully.

Seth Godin gets at this in his unique way when he offers,

> Our society is struggling because during times of change, the very last people you need on your team are well-paid bureau-

crats, note takers, literalists, manual readers, TGIF laborers, map followers, and fearful employees. The compliant masses don't help so much when you don't know what to do next. . . . Some organizations haven't realized this yet, or haven't articulated it, but we need artists. Artists are people with a genius for finding a new answer, a new connection, or a new way of getting things done.

He makes a distinction between a factory worker, who for me represents the prosaic past, and the artist, who represents the poetic future. A great example is the difference between a cook and a chef. The cook just follows a recipe to cook something. The chef digs deep into her soul and creates something beautiful. One works in prose. The other is a poet, an artist.

I remember the best hamburger I ever ate. Actually, that I ever *experienced*. My friend Dave Wright—or Super Dave, as his friends call him—hosted Sharon and me in a lovely home on the shores of Lake Michigan for a few memorable summer days several years ago. Dave is a chef by avocation. For pleasure he takes time off of his real job in vocational ministry to cook in five-star restaurants. One evening we watched him cook a hamburger that was an absolute work of art. Really. I can no more explain how he did what he did than I can explain Picasso. But I do know that the final product was garnished with a slice of Granny Smith apple and a sauce of some angelic origin. Years later I can still see, smell, and taste that meal. We didn't just eat it. We experienced it. This is what an artist does.

> Hospitable communicators . . . do not just attempt to say a thing; we work hard to say it artfully.

Hospitable communicators are artists. We create experiences that convey beauty and stir hearts. Eugene Peterson is probably best known for his translation of the Bible, *The Message*. I have been most affected, however, by his observations on being a pastor, leader, writer, and speaker. His insights are a revelation for any leader who strives to be a hospitable communicator. In his memoir, *The Pastor*, he wrote that he worked hard to "understand the sacred qualities of language." He gave sage advice from his personal history as a communicator:

> I started paying attention to poets and novelists and artists, the way they wrote about what they were doing as writers and musicians and painters, weavers and potters and sculptors. I made friends with the world of art, the work of the artist. I embraced artists as allies. They took a place alongside the theologians and biblical scholars in my formation: art as a school of pastoral formation, the pastor as artist. My artistic medium was words, written and prayed and preached.

Again, hospitable communicators are artists.

To communicate beauty, we must fill our minds with the beautiful. To save ourselves from the boring prose of an unimaginative mind, we must explore the minds of those who stir up our imaginations—those who have created great books, poetry, paintings, pictures, movies. The older I get, the more I appreciate exploring the mind of God by immersing myself in the world *He* created. The apostle Paul said that we can get to know God through His creation. Oceans, mountains, sunsets, forests. To use Peterson's beautifully crafted translation in Philippians 4, "Summing it all up, friends, I'd say you'll do best by filling your minds and meditating on things true, noble, reputable, authentic, compelling, gracious—the best, not the worst; the beautiful, not the ugly; things to praise, not things to curse." We must fill our minds with the beautiful in order to artistically convey the beautiful.

As important as words are, though, we must also remember that communication is about much more than words. Ken

Gire expressed that "words are often the least effective way of communicating." Who can really describe the appearance or fragrance of a rose? You have to see it and smell it to understand it. It's like the ballerina who was asked to explain what a particular dance meant. She replied, "If I could have said it, I wouldn't have needed to dance it."

Since I am a speaker and writer—a words person—I know I need to surround myself with people who have communicative gifts that make my words more effective, or who simply communicate things so well that sometimes I don't need to say anything at all. Thank God for architects and landscapers; for scriptwriters, directors, and editors; for florists, decorators, and event planners; for lyricists, singers, and musicians; for photographers and graphic artists. I love collaborating with people who use their gifts to foster beautiful communicative environments where people's hearts can be warmed to receive something good and true.

I have to frequently remind myself that beauty—at least the beauty humans create—is not about perfection. I am a recovering perfectionist. I have learned that perfectionism damages the soul and kills creativity. We must strive for excellence, of course, but a standard of perfection may mean that we never offer anything at all.

Nicholas Wilton, the founder of Artplane, imagines that someone once organized everything in the world into categories that made sense. After putting everything that made sense into its perfect place, there was a bunch of stuff that was left over. In frustration, this organizer threw everything that did not fit into a big box and labeled it ART. Wilton then writes,

> Art, among all the other tidy categories, most closely resembles what it is like to be human. To be alive. It is our nature to be

imperfect. To have uncategorized feelings and emotions. To make or do things that don't sometimes necessarily make sense. Art is all just perfectly imperfect.

Once the word *Art* enters the description of what you're up to, it is almost like getting a hall pass from perfection. It thankfully releases us from any expectation of perfection.

We should all be set free from the toxic thinking that keeps us from wholeheartedly doing our best to create beauty because we think it has to be perfect.

I think a good word to contrast against perfection is the word *authentic*. I once had a beautiful Fender Stratocaster guitar. It was nicked and scratched from use and travel. It was not perfect. But it was authentic. Authentic, in this regard, is better than perfect. We communicate the good and beautiful from what is true in the depths of our soul. Again, we must strive for excellence, but the beauty we create begins in our authentic selves—not our perfect selves.

I have learned over the years that people tend to receive authenticity as beauty. When we communicate from who we really are, it pleases something in people's souls. It's like the multi-Grammy-award-winning hip-hop/R&B superstar who asked me to celebrate the fifteen-year renewal of his wedding vows, a huge—and extravagantly expensive—event for him and his wife. He wanted to send his tailor to make me a suit that would match his suit and the suit of the other men in his wedding party. The suit was not me. I said, hospitably, "No." When the big day arrived, I showed up at the venue dressed in the well-tailored—but by his standards boring—suit that I typically do weddings in. I was led to where he was waiting. He stood there, drink in hand, surrounded by his entourage. As I approached, he lowered his sunglasses and looked me up and down. Then he said in a hip-hop kind of way, "You look coo', that's why you my pastor." Well, I have seldom been accused of being "coo'."

Or cool. But somehow I was cool to him because I am just who I am. And somehow, though he is from a totally different world than I am in almost every way, he connects to that and receives what I wholeheartedly offer.

I am trying to say that people find authenticity beautiful and that when we try to do beautiful things out of a sincere heart, people respond to who we are. They resonate. Fyodor Dostoyevsky described a woman who had aged, yet channeled beauty from deep in her heart:

> Her face still kept the remnants of its former beauty, and be-sides, she looked much younger than her age, as almost always happens with women who keep their clarity of spirit, the fresh-ness of their impressions, and the honest, pure ardor of their hearts into old age. Let us say parenthetically that keeping all this is the only means of preserving one's beauty even in old age. Her hair was already thinning and starting to turn gray, little radiating wrinkles had long since appeared around her eyes, her cheeks were sunken and dry from worry and grief, and still her face was beautiful.

This woman was beautiful because of who she was. Beauty begins in our soul.

I intend to do everything in my power to create communica-tive environments that are pleasing to people's physical senses. I intend to imagine and work and sacrifice to make that happen. I know that my every effort to communicate meaningful things— useful things—is more effective in any setting of beauty. But I will also remember that cultivating authenticity in my soul, and communicating out of who I am, is more important than any other attempt to do any beautiful thing. The woman who did a beautiful thing for Jesus offered more than an expensive bottle and fragrant perfume; she offered her heart. Who she was, was beautiful.

The truest inner beauty can only come by God's grace. Each of us who are children of God are indwelled by "the beauty of the Lord." And more than anything else, that provides the basis for truly hospitable communication. Because of this beauty endowed by God, we all can—if we want to—do beautiful things that honor God and lead people to something more.

Leadership Take-Homes

1. **Beauty is integral to hospitable communicative environments.** Many times, doing a beautiful thing—even an extravagant gesture—is the best way to also do a good and useful thing.

2. **Hospitable communicators are artists who create experiences that convey beauty and stir hearts.** We do not just attempt to say something, we work hard to say it artfully, beautifully.

3. **The beauty we must create is not about perfection.** Cultivating authenticity in our soul and communicating out of who we really are is beautiful.

Sources

"Why are you bothering this woman?": Matthew 26:10–11.
"She has done a beautiful thing": Matthew 26:10.
"She has done a good work": Matthew 26:10 NKJV.
"She has done a good deed.": Matthew 26:10 NASB.
"introduces us to emotions": Ken Gire, *Windows of the Soul* (Grand Rapids: Zondervan, 1996), 84.
"every man is almost always led to believe": Douglas Wilson and Douglas Jones, *Angels in the Architecture: A Protestant Vision for Middle Earth* (Moscow, ID: Canon Press, 1998), 21.

"to find the place where": C.S. Lewis, *Till We Have Faces* (San Diego: Harvest Books, 1980), 74.

"includes the notion of 'call'": John O'Donohue, *The Invisible Embrace of Beauty* (New York: Harper, 2005), 19–20.

"we would understand": Wilson and Jones, *Angels in the Architecture*, 28, 31.

"Too late came I to love thee": Wilson and Jones, 25.

"Let the beauty of the Lord": Psalm 90:17 KJV.

"We don't make 'automobiles'": Daniel H. Pink, *A Whole New Mind* (New York: Penguin Group, 2005), 79.

A politician should campaign in poetry but govern in prose.: Elizabeth Kolbert, "Postscript: Mario Cuomo (1932-2015)," *The New Yorker*, January 2015, www.newyorker.com/news/news-desk/postscript-mario-cuomo.

"About the great events": James Sire, *How to Read Slowly* (Wheaton: Harold Shaw, 1978), 58.

"Our society is struggling": Seth Godin, *Linchpin* (New York: Penguin, 2010), 7.

"understand the sacred qualities": Eugene Peterson, *The Pastor* (New York: Harper Collins, 2011), 239–240.

The apostle Paul said that we can get to know God: Romans 1:19–20.

"Summing it all up, friends": Philippians 4:8–9 MESSAGE.

"words are often the least effective way": Ken Gire, *Windows of the Soul* (Grand Rapids: Zondervan, 1996), 148.

"Art, among all the other tidy categories": Nicholas Wilton as quoted by Brené Brown in *Daring Greatly: How the Courage to Be Vulnerable Transforms the Way We Live, Love, Parent, and Lead* (New York: Avery, 2012), 136.

"Her face still kept the remnants": Fyodor Dostoyevsky, *Crime and Punishment* (New York: Vintage, 1992), 206.

"the beauty of the Lord.": Psalm 90:17 KJV.

FEASTS

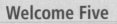

12

Enjoy Life

Many years ago I had an epiphany of sorts that altered my basic state of being in ways that I now know were necessary for me to have the potential to become a hospitable leader. It's kind of a fun story, I think.

It started with a trip to the mall with my three then-young children, to buy gifts for their mother very late in the Christmas season. Thankfully, Sumerr and Caleb quickly found gifts they could purchase with their allowance money—and a little help from Dad—that they thought their mom would enjoy. Christian, the youngest, had no such luck. So he ended up buying—at my urging—a desperation gift displayed in the checkout line at Restoration Hardware of all places. It was a book about how to defeat incivility by returning to the simple courtesies that build community. Like manners. It's called *Say Please, Say Thank You: The Respect We Owe One Another.* Sharon loves—loves!—good manners, and we were in a hurry, so we grabbed a book at a hardware store. I thought that was that.

Much to my surprise, Sharon raved about this book as she began reading it. And she kept insisting on reading parts of it to me. Frankly, I had no interest in her hardware-store book on manners and kept politely avoiding her attempts to make it an audiobook just for me. Then one evening, on our way home from a family ski day in the mountains of North Jersey, the five of us were in a restaurant sitting around a table covered with an abundance of food and drink. Sharon pulled this book out of her purse and said she was going to read to us from it and that we were all going to listen. She began with a section about the joy of shared meals:

> Of all the wonderful gifts of the Creator, near the top of the list is the joy of eating. God, I presume, could have made us with neither the biological necessity nor the aesthetic pleasure of consuming nourishment. But I don't think it's entirely metaphorical when the Psalmist says, "Taste and see that the Lord is good." Take a bite of well-made pizza, covered with sausage and artichoke hearts and mushrooms, and follow it with a swallow of fine Cabernet, with hints of blackberry and spice and vanilla, and meditate on the exquisite explosion of sensations on your palette. . . . If you are of the reductionist "food is fuel" school . . . It's never too late for repentance . . . and I beg you to return from the far country of ingratitude to enjoy the full feast of life.

Now she had my attention. Here our family sat at that table enjoying a feast together, listening to her read about the feast of life. By the time she got to a section on the glories of hollandaise, I was mesmerized:

> If you prepare a meal for me, it's my responsibility—my solemn *duty*—to enjoy it. . . . moderation is called for in all things, including zealotry in diet. Robert Capon . . . puts it this way: "Food these days is often identified as the enemy. Butter, salt, sugar, eggs, are all out to get you. And yet at our best we know better. Butter is . . . well, butter: it glorifies almost everything it touches. Salt is the sovereign of all flavors. Eggs are, pure and

simple, one of the wonders of the world. And if you put them altogether, you get not a sudden death, but hollandaise—which in its own way is not one less bit a marvel than the Gothic arch, the computer chip, or a Bach fugue."

I said, "Wow. That's great writing. Sounds a little hedonistic, though." And I'm a little embarrassed to admit this, but I added, "I bet the guy who wrote this is obese." Sharon replied, "Actually, he's a pastor. And he looks like he is in fine shape." She showed me the picture of a fit-looking middle-aged guy. And then I realized that I recognized him. Donald McCullough had written a book on holiness that had really impacted my life some years earlier called *The Trivialization of God*. I had been so affected by it that I preached a long series on repentance to my congregation. Really.

The Trivialization of God opens like this: "Visit a church on Sunday morning—almost any will do—and . . . you will not likely find much awe or sense of mystery. . . . Reverence and awe have often been replaced by a yawn of familiarity. The consuming fire has been domesticated into a candle flame . . . it may well be revealed that the worst sin of the church at the end of the 20th century has been the trivialization of God."

When I realized that the same person had written both books, I was temporarily confused. How can the same guy write so eloquently about holiness—and the glories of butter?

Then came my epiphany: Holiness and hollandaise are not mutually exclusive. And a lot of things that I had been thinking about for a long time somehow came together in that moment. Particularly something Jesus said about himself: "The Son of Man came eating and drinking, and they say 'Here is a glutton and a drunkard,'" or as another translation has it, "The Son of Man came, enjoying life."

Here was Jesus—the holiest man who ever lived, doing the most consequential work in the history of the world: enjoying life to such an apparent excess that His enemies accused Him of being a drunkard and a glutton. It's important to note that *He* said He came "eating and drinking," but *they* said he was "a drunkard and a glutton." He openly acknowledged the feast part but clearly was not abusing food or drink. He was without sin, and drunkenness and gluttony are, of course, sins. The larger point is that in Jesus, holiness and hollandaise met. Or more accurately, as the psalmist prophesied, in Jesus, "Mercy and truth have met together; righteousness and peace have kissed."

You may rightfully ask, "What in the world does this have to do with leadership?" I humbly suggest that it has everything to do with leadership, at least if one wants to be a hospitable leader. You may remember that in the first chapter of this book I wrote that Jesus described His kingdom as a wedding feast that a king prepared for his son. It's crazy that the most successful leader who ever lived described His rule in terms of a feast. This is not a minor theme in the Jesus story. History as we know it wraps up with a feast called the Wedding Supper of the Lamb. Isaiah described the state of things in the world to come—a world made possible by the leadership of Jesus—like this: "On this mountain the Lord Almighty will prepare a feast of rich food for all peoples, a banquet of aged wine—the best of meats and the finest of wines."

> **Hospitable leadership should feel like a feast to those who are being led.**

Hospitable leadership should feel like a feast to those who are being led. And if we are going to create an environment like that, we who are leading are going to have to accept the invitation Jesus offers us to feast with Him. He essentially told us that the kingdom of God is like a great banquet and everyone is invited. We must experience the feast of life if we are going to throw a feast for those we hope to lead.

<hr/>

"Work is either fun or drudgery. It depends on your attitude. I like fun," said Colleen Barrett, former CEO and current president emeritus of Southwest Airlines. One of Southwest's three core values is "a fun-LUVing attitude." It's no wonder that so many customers are so loyal to Southwest and that employee turnover is so ridiculously low. This airline does a lot of things well, but doing a lot of things well in an environment where people are enjoying life and work is most assuredly a force multiplier.

I like the story in which Barrett's predecessor as CEO of Southwest, Herb Kelleher, received a complaint letter from an irate customer: A flight attendant had made the pre-flight safety announcements and said something to the effect of, "In the unlikely event of a water landing, your flight attendant will come by with drinks and a towel." Some humorless customer didn't think that was funny at all—and she let Kelleher know it. His response to the angry letter from this customer was a three-word letter: "We'll miss you."

You have to love this for so many reasons, but especially because creating "a fun-LUVing" culture is so important to Southwest that organizational leaders are willing to stand behind employees who actually live out this value. What a marvelous thing for leaders to consistently message to everyone in their sphere of influence that "we are serious about having fun here." One could argue that creating this kind of environment is essential to leading a healthy organization that encourages the health of those who people it. "A cheerful heart is good medicine, but a crushed spirit dries up the bones."

Our leadership sphere can hardly feel like a feast, however, if the leader is not enjoying life. We simply must learn how to have fun in order to create an environment of fun. We must learn to recline at life's banquet table in order to invite those we lead to experience what we are leading as a celebration.

This—our need to enjoy life—may seem obvious on its face. For many of us, however, it's more difficult than it seems. I heard Tim Ferriss speak for many of us in a recent podcast when he said, "If we are a type A personality, if we have competed in school, competed in X, competed in Y and Z, we are trained by ourselves to believe that if we are not redlining, if we are not overcome with effort, that we are not doing a good job. We are not trying hard enough. I often think that leads us to seek complicated paths with many, many moving pieces." It's as though, if we are really serious about success and significance and moving our mission forward, we are inclined to be unrelentingly hard on ourselves. When we do have fun it's compartmentalized, meaning that work is serious and consumes most of our lives and then we guiltily sneak times to have fun in the non-work segments of our lives. To think about leading in a context that feels like a feast, I suspect, is a challenging paradigm shift for many of us.

The difference in the lifestyle and leadership approach of Jesus and John the Baptist is instructive for me in this regard. When Jesus said that He came "enjoying life," He was responding to a message from John the Baptist, who was in prison and had heard about all the things the Messiah was doing. John had sent his disciples to ask Jesus, "Are you the Messiah we've been expecting, or should we keep looking for someone else?" Jesus replied to John's questions by giving him several reasons John should trust that he had been correct when he introduced Jesus as the One the world had been waiting for. And then Jesus spoke about John and the singular role he had played in history as the forerunner of Jesus. He said that no one who had ever lived was greater than John the Baptist.

But Jesus went on to make a dramatic statement that contrasted the manner in which He and John had come to do ministry. He said that John's preaching was more like the songs you would sing at a funeral and that His own was more like the songs you would sing at a wedding feast. "'We played wedding songs, and you didn't dance, so we played funeral songs, and you didn't mourn.' For John didn't spend his time eating and drinking, and you say, 'He's possessed by a demon.' The Son of Man, on the other hand, feasts and drinks, and you say, 'He's a glutton and a drunkard, and a friend of tax collectors and other sinners!' But wisdom is shown to be right by its results." Wait a minute. Did I just say that Jesus compared John the Baptist's lifestyle and leadership to a funeral? Yes, I did.

Jesus introduced a new manner of living and leading in every way. Remember that John was the last prophet of the law. Jesus initiated a new era: grace. "Until John the Baptist, the law of Moses and the messages of the prophets were your guides. But now the Good News of the Kingdom of God is preached, and everyone is eager to get in."

John lived an ascetic life, dwelling in the wilderness and existing on a diet of locusts and wild honey. As a Nazirite, no razor ever touched his head. He dressed in burlap. His communication style was full of truth . . . but without grace. It's a stretch to imagine John or his disciples having a lot of fun. It's fascinating to me that John began losing some of his followers to Jesus while they were doing ministry contemporaneously.

"The next day John was there again with two of his disciples. When he saw Jesus passing by, he said, 'Look, the Lamb of God!' When the two disciples heard him say this, they followed Jesus. Turning around, Jesus saw them following and asked, 'What do you want?' They said, 'Rabbi' (which means "Teacher"), 'where are you staying?' 'Come,' he replied, 'and you will see.' So they went and saw where he was staying, and they spent that day with him."

On another occasion, while Jesus was at a dinner party with His disciples, "John's disciples came and asked him, 'How is it that we and the Pharisees fast often, but your disciples do not fast?' Jesus answered, 'How can the guests of the bridegroom mourn while he is with them? The time will come when the bridegroom will be taken from them; then they will fast.'"

Solely from a leadership perspective, who would you rather follow, John or Jesus? I think it's safe to say most people would rather follow Jesus. Which begs the question: Whose leadership does yours resemble more in terms of overall environment? Jesus' or John's? Grace or law? Enjoying life or . . . ?

John was a law man. His job was to tell people where they had fallen short and to prepare them for Jesus. The law is a schoolmaster that leads us to grace. But it is not supposed to be our normal state. We are to live in a state of grace.

I think that the human default position is law. We have an innate desire to earn our way to acceptance. To do enough. To be good enough. To be worthy enough. Even though I know I am accepted by God through faith and by grace, I sometimes have a challenge living—and leading—gracefully. I still get messages from that figurative prison: "How can you be the real deal if you are enjoying life?" It's as though it has to be hard, and if it's not hard, I can't be happy. This kind of emotional/spiritual state leaks out into our leadership and creates an inhospitable environment. And remember that the law—the letter—kills people. Law-based leadership fosters an environment that feels like a funeral. But Jesus invites us to feast. If I am to be a hospitable leader, I simply must learn to feast like Jesus.

Enjoying the good and beautiful things in this world does not make us worldly or even something less than serious. If I am not careful I can slip into a subtle Gnosticism. The Gnostics believed that matter was inherently evil—and that spirituality could only be attained by a denial of the physical world. One of the major battles in early Christianity was against Gnosticism.

The Gnostics denied the incarnation. They could not accept that God would manifest himself in matter. We know, however, that in Jesus God was not only wrapped in flesh, but enjoyed life and fully embraced the human experience.

Obviously there is a time for fasting and the practicing of other spiritual disciplines that deny our human appetites and help to satisfy the hunger of our spirits. Most of us easily associate spirituality and a seriousness of purpose with spiritual disciplines. I just wonder if we miss how important celebration is to what it means to live and lead like Jesus. We should be intentional about fasting and we should also be intentional about feasting. In his classic *Celebration of Discipline*, Richard Foster warned us:

> It is an occupational hazard of devout folk to become stuffy bores. This should not be. Of all people we should be the most free, alive, interesting. Celebration adds a note of gaiety, festivity, hilarity to our lives. . . . Now I am not recommending a periodic romp in sin, but I am suggesting that we do need deeper, more earthy experiences of exhilaration. It is healing and refreshing to cultivate a wide appreciation for life. Our spirit can become weary with straining after God just as our body can become weary with overwork. Celebration helps us to relax and enjoy the good things of the earth.

It is interesting to note that I often read the life stories of some of the men and women I most admire in history—people I would think of in terms of holiness—and find that there was no conflict in their lives between serious work and enjoying the pleasures of life. Like C.S. Lewis, who saw the good and beautiful pleasures of this world as "the drippings of grace." As Philip Yancey wrote, "Lewis saw no need to withdraw from the world and shun pleasure. He loved a stiff drink, a puff on the pipe, a gathering of friends, a Shakespeare play, a witty joke." Now, some of us may not particularly appreciate a Shakespearean play. Some of us might not want to—or simply shouldn't—get within a mile of a stiff drink, perhaps because our view of Scripture or our conscience would not allow it, or because we know we would abuse it, or maybe because we just don't like the stuff. That's not the point. The point is that we all need to find our own way to experience pleasure in the context of holiness as "the drippings of grace."

This brings to mind something else Jesus said to John the Baptist. When John sent his disciples to query Jesus after he "heard all the things the Messiah was doing," Jesus encouraged John that "God blesses those who are not offended by me." Maybe we ought to have just enough fun that the legalist imprisoned within us gets a wee bit offended at times. Come on. The kingdom of God is like a feast a king threw for his son.

Dietrich Bonhoeffer was an eloquent spokesman for a serious Christianity. He wrote brilliantly about *The Cost of Discipleship*. He was so dedicated to righteousness that he was one of the few German clergymen to stand against Hitler in both words and actions. And he ended up being executed for it. Yet he had a deep appreciation for the innocent pleasures of life: "At the heart of Bonhoeffer's theology was the mystery of the incarnation. . . . It was because of this that he embraced the humanity of Jesus Christ in the way that religious pietists could not, and it was because of this that he felt justified in embracing the good things of this world as gifts from the hand of God, rather than as temptations to be avoided. So even in prison, Bonhoeffer's enjoyment of people and life was very much alive."

While he was in prison, his family would turn their visits into celebrations. They brought him gifts including a floral arrangement, pieces of art, an expensive wristwatch, a family heirloom that had once belonged to writer and philosopher Goethe, and a cigar—a gift from the great theologian Karl Barth. I am reminded of Paul's admonition to Timothy, "Command those who are rich in this present world . . . to put their hope in God, who richly provides us with everything for our enjoyment."

There is an insightful passage in Deuteronomy where God commanded His people to put aside some of their income to provide for a meal that was to be enjoyed in God's presence. Here is part of what it says: "Use the silver to buy whatever you like: cattle, sheep, wine or other fermented drink, or anything you wish. Then you and your household shall eat there in the presence of the Lord your God and rejoice." God commanded His people to feast in His presence. To which I say we must learn to invest in and be intentional about enjoying life in the presence of the Lord. Enjoy beautiful art in the presence of the Lord. Dance to an inspiring song in the presence of the Lord. Eat a bountiful meal in the presence of the Lord. Watch a great Broadway show in the presence of the Lord. Play golf in the presence of the Lord. Enjoy nature in the presence of the Lord. Enjoy the intimacies of marriage in the presence of the Lord. Enjoy life in the presence of the Lord your God and rejoice!

We must learn to invest in and be intentional about enjoying life.

Enjoying the feast of life is part of holiness. It's like Nehemiah and his leadership team said to the people who felt condemned when they heard God's Word and became aware of how far they fell short of God's best for their lives. Nehemiah called them to repentance. He also told them to "'Go and enjoy choice food and sweet drinks, and send some to those who have nothing prepared. This day is holy to our Lord. Do not grieve, for the joy of the Lord is your strength.' The Levites calmed all the people, saying, 'Be still, for this is a holy day. Do not grieve.' Then all the people went away to eat and drink, to send portions of food and to celebrate with great joy. . . .'" This is at least part of how we should think about a life of holiness.

I am so serious about my work—and so intent on being a great leader—that I know I simply must get better at enjoying life. I am not talking about mind-numbing escapism or an immoderate lifestyle that is unserious and brings destruction. I am talking about making certain my approach to life includes enjoying the good, beautiful, and innocent pleasures God so richly provides. I want everyone in my sphere of influence to feel like they have been invited to a great feast, especially as we invest our lives in a great cause. It may sound a little sappy, but I wonder if people in today's crazy, inhospitable world aren't longing for something similar to the desire expressed in the Song of Songs: "Let him lead me to the banquet hall, and let his banner over me be love." That's what Jesus did. And that's what I want to do. This is quintessential hospitable leadership.

Leadership Take-Homes

1. **Embrace the feast of life.** We must allow ourselves to enjoy life in order for our leadership to feel like a feast.

2. **Grace-full leadership trumps law-based leadership.** Jesus was a grace-full leader while John the Baptist was a law-based leader. Who would you rather follow? Whose leadership style does yours most resemble?

3. **Enjoying the good and beautiful things in this world does not make us worldly or unserious.** Jesus came enjoying life yet did the most important work in history.

Sources

"Of all the wonderful gifts of the Creator": Donald McCullough, *Say Please, Say Thank You* (New York: G.P. Putnam's Sons, 1998), 57–58.

"If you prepare a meal for me": McCullough, *Say Please, Say Thank You,* 59–60.

"Visit a church on Sunday": Donald McCullough, *The Trivialization of God: The Dangerous Illusion of a Manageable Deity* (Colorado Springs: NavPress, 1995), 13.

"The Son of Man came eating": Matthew 11:19.

"The Son of Man came, enjoying life": Matthew 11:19 PHILLIPS.

"Mercy and truth have met together": Psalm 85:10 NKJV.

"On this mountain the Lord Almighty": Isaiah 25:6.

the kingdom of God is like: Luke 14:15–23.

"Work is either fun or drudgery.": Colleen Barrett, former CEO of Southwest Airlines, http://www.famous-quotes-and-quotations.com/colleen_c_barrett.html

"We'll miss you.": Patrick Lencioni, *The Advantage* (San Francisco: Jossey-Bass, 2012), 94–95.

"A cheerful heart is good medicine": Proverbs 17:22.

"If we are a type A personality": Tim Ferriss, *The Tim Ferriss Show.*

"enjoying life": Matthew 11:19 PHILLIPS.

"John the Baptist": Matthew 11:2–3 NLT.

"We played wedding songs": Matthew 11:17–19 NLT.

"Until John the Baptist": Luke 16:16 NLT.

"The next day John was there": John 1:35–39.

"John's disciples came and asked": Matthew 9:14–15.

John was a law man. . . . The law is a schoolmaster: Galatians 3:24 KJV.

the letter—kills people: 2 Corinthians 3:6.

"it is an occupational hazard": Richard Foster, *Celebration of Discipline: The Path to Spiritual Growth* (New York: HarperCollins, 1998), 168.

"the drippings of grace": Philip Yancey, *What Good Is God* (New York: FaithWords-Hachette, 2010), 101.

"Lewis saw no need": Philip Yancey, *What Good is God,* 101.

"God blesses those who are not offended by me": Matthew 11:6 NLT (1996).

"At the heart of Bonhoeffer's theology": Eric Metaxas, *Bonhoeffer* (Nashville: Thomas Nelson, 2010), 472–473.

While he was in prison, his family: Eric Metaxas, *Bonhoeffer,* 473.

"Command those who are rich": 1 Timothy 6:17.

"Use the silver to buy whatever": Deuteronomy 14:26.

"Go and enjoy": Nehemiah 8:10–12.

"Let him lead me to the banquet hall": Song of Songs 2:4.

13

Happiness Creates Conditions for Success

I submit that it is my solemn obligation to be happy. Especially if I want to be a successful leader. Robert Lewis Stevenson had it right when he said, "There is no duty we so much underrate as the duty of being happy." Someone told a friend of mine that I was talking a lot about happiness these days. His response was incredulity: "He is emphasizing happiness?" I laughed when I heard that. And I get it. My personality is more driver than sanguine. I am more suited to be a football coach than a cheerleader. I am not given to lighthearted frivolity. I am given to setting goals, and getting better, and making a difference, and measurable outcomes, and as soon as possible, if you please. Maybe just a little intense. Which is exactly why I am writing about happiness. I have become utterly convinced that one of the great secrets of living a life of meaning and accomplishment is to live in a manner that promotes happiness.

Until recent years I simply undervalued happiness. I did not focus on what a big deal it is that God is happy and invites me to share in His happiness. Jesus referred to this when He told a story where He intimated that the reward for a life well lived would include God saying, "Come and share your master's happiness!"

I can't help but be reminded of a well-known passage in Dallas Willard's classic *Divine Conspiracy*. "We should . . . think that God leads a very interesting life, and that he is full of joy. Undoubtedly he is the most joyous being in the universe." Willard wrote of a time when he came upon a scene in nature so stunning that words could not capture his elation: "Gradually there crept into my mind the realization that God sees this all the time. . . . Great tidal waves of joy must constantly wash through his being . . . Suddenly I was extremely happy for God and thought I had some sense of what an infinitely joyous consciousness he is. . . ." And then he finished with the statement that "he is simply one great inexhaustible and eternal experience of all that is good and true and beautiful and right. This is what we must think of when we hear theologians and philosophers speak of him as a perfect being. This is his life."

> Happiness is a precursor to success—not a result of success.

The apostle Paul captured God's happy condition when he invoked "the glory of the blessed God" or "blissful God" or "happy God." God is happy in spite of everything He has been through. Happy is God's state of being. And He invites us to share in His happiness. I am determined to say yes to His invitation.

God made us to be happy. Scientific research reveals that happiness is a powerful predictor of achievement. Happy people simply have stunning advantages in life and are more likely to realize their God-given potential than people who are discontent. Happiness is a precursor to success—not a result of success. Think about it like this: Money doesn't buy you happiness, but happiness may "buy" you money. Now apply this to things much more important than money. What do I mean? Happiness creates the conditions for success.

A compilation of nearly every study about happiness ever conducted—over two hundred studies involving 275,000 people worldwide—disclosed mind-boggling results. "Happiness leads to success in nearly every domain, including work, health, friendship, sociability, creativity and energy." Some of these studies are crazy. One reveals that happy doctors make a correct diagnosis much faster and display more creativity in treatments than doctors in a neutral state of mind. *The Harvard Business Review* focused an entire double issue on the economic value of happiness, showing among other findings that happy people in business produce higher profits and that there is a correlation—probably a causation—between higher happiness levels among citizens in a nation and a higher gross domestic product. Another study detailed that "how happy individuals were as college freshmen predicted how high their income was nineteen years later, regardless of their initial level of wealth." Study after study divulges that happy people are healthier and live longer, more satisfying lives.

As in most everything else, the happiness stakes are dramatically higher for a leader because leaders have the power to create conditions for others. Hospitable leaders must be happy people, and in our happiness we must create environments that are conducive to inspiring happiness in the people we lead.

Emotions—both positive and negative—are contagious. Research shows that we are all formidably affected by the emotional state of those we spend time with. Even strangers transmit their moods to one another after being in a room together for just a few minutes. Imagine the impact our state of being has on those we are living and working with every day.

If we are unhappy, our melancholy leaks and affects those around us. Daniel Goleman wrote, "Like secondhand smoke, the leakage of emotions can make a bystander an innocent casualty of someone else's toxic state." It saddens me—pun intended—to think that my bad mood can make the people around me sad. It's like there should be a baseline leadership oath: "First, do no harm." I must realize that if I am unhappy— especially as a leader, a parent, a teacher, a manager, a coach—I am doing damage to the people around me.

Thankfully, positive emotions exude as well. The happier you are, the happier the people around you will be. And as the acclaimed expert in the science of happiness Shawn Achor wrote, "The power to spark emotional contagion multiplies if you are in a leadership position. Studies have found that when leaders are in a positive mood, their employees are more likely to be in a positive mood themselves, to exhibit prosocial helping behaviors toward one another, and to coordinate tasks more efficiently and with less effort." I must be happy if only because it helps the people around me be happier and more successful in their lives. One could argue that if I am not happy, I commit leadership malpractice.

I read a fascinating—and kind of bizarre—article about how some sports teams have begun hiring facial coding experts to study the expressions of players to determine whether they have the right emotional attributes to help their teams win. The title of the article is pretty self-explanatory: "Teams Turn to a Face Reader, Looking for that Winning Smile." One talented NBA player was deemed too sad to lead his team effectively because "sadness as an emotion tends to slow you down both physically and mentally, not a good thing in the flexible give and take sport of basketball." Another player who was having a great year showed "enough 'true' smiles, which equate to joy and contribute to what has been a highly effective season." What would happen if an expert was able to look at your face and determine your level of happiness? Imagine something like this: "John is too sad to be a great father because sadness tends to limit a father's effectiveness." Or, "Olivia is too unhappy to be a great teacher because unhappiness creates a climate in the classroom that makes it difficult for kids to learn." Or, "Andre's discontentment in his present position in this company makes it difficult to promote him to the position he says he wants because a sense of optimism is necessary for success at the next level."

We often think that happiness is the result of something good happening to us. And it is true that having good things happen can increase happiness. But it is even more often true that good things happen to us because we are happy. It stands to reason, for instance, that a happy person would help create a happy marriage rather than an unhappy person being made happy by a happy marriage. Or that a happy entrepreneur would create a business that increases her happiness rather than an unhappy person becoming happy because of a successful business. Happiness is having the horse before the cart.

Are you too sad to be an effective leader? As leaders we have an ethical responsibility to lead ourselves to happiness and to create the conditions where good things are more likely to happen to us and those we lead.

One of the great fallacies is that we will be happy when something we want to happen does in fact happen: when we get married, when we have kids, when we have a certain amount of money or achieve certain goals. As if happiness is a result of what we have or have accomplished.

In the tenth century, Abd Al-Rahman III was the absolute ruler of Córdoba in Spain. He seemed to have everything anyone could think of having. Toward the end of his life he wrote that he had reigned for more than fifty years and was loved by his subjects, feared by his enemies, and respected by his allies. "Riches and honors, power and pleasure, have waited on my call, nor does any earthly blessing appear to have been wanting to my felicity." Sounds pretty good, right? But he continues, "I have diligently numbered the days of pure and genuine happiness which have fallen to my lot: they amount to 14." What? A long life—apparently everything one could want—and only fourteen days of pure and genuine happiness. What makes a person happy? Evidently more than riches, honors, powers, and pleasure. And evidently more than achieving and having a lot of the things that many of us have thought would make us happy.

So, what is happiness? I believe happiness is the pleasure we feel when we live our lives today and imagine our futures in light of ultimate meaning. And I believe that having hope—hope that our lives have a purpose that is being worked out in view of eternal meaning—is the secret to happiness.

> Having hope—hope that our lives have a purpose that is being worked out in view of eternal meaning—is the secret to happiness.

Dr. Tal Ben-Shahar, who launched the wildly popular Happiness course at Harvard University, defines happiness as "the overall experience of pleasure and meaning." He writes, "A happy person enjoys positive emotions while perceiving her life as purposeful." Shawn Achor concludes that happiness is "pleasure combined with deeper feelings of meaning and purpose. Happiness implies a positive mood in the present and a positive outlook for the future." I don't think that happiness is primarily the euphoric high we feel when we experience pleasurable things, though I am all for that. The happiness I want to experience—and that I want you to experience—is a constant state of being. It's the pleasure we feel when we think about our lives in light of our life's purpose. It's how we feel in the big picture of a life full of meaning. Happiness is the aggregate of our experiences coupled with our positive expectations about the future. It's a yes answer to the question "Are you happy?"

I suggest that two thousand years ago the apostle Paul nailed this happiness thing when he wrote the following words to Christ-followers living in Rome in the first century: "Since we have been made right with God by our faith, we have peace with God. This happened through our Lord Jesus Christ, who through our faith has brought us into that blessing of God's grace that we now enjoy. And we are happy because of the hope we have of sharing God's glory." Let's break this down. First, Paul said that through Jesus we have peace with God. This peace is related to the Hebrew concept of shalom, which we have discussed, and which intimates that we have oneness with God and experience "absolute wholeness—full, harmonious, joyful, flourishing life." When we have peace with God, everything in our lives should work the way God designed it to work. And note . . . we are to enjoy this now. "This happened through our Lord Jesus Christ, who through our faith has brought us into that blessing of God's grace that we now enjoy." I believe with all my heart that this restored relationship with God is the basis for meaning.

But my focus here—and in the next chapter—is on what Paul wrote next: "and we are happy because of the hope we have of sharing God's glory." Having hope in light of God's glory is truly pleasure in view of purpose. If we do not have hope for today and for our futures, aligned with what life fundamentally means, then "we are the most miserable people in the world."

God's glory has to do with who He is—and what He does—and His purposes being worked out in and through us and His world. God's glory refers to ultimate meaning. No wonder translators have struggled to find a word that describes the state of pleasure that is found and the happiness that results because of the hope we have of sharing God's glory. We are "happy" or "rejoice" or "exult" as we "confidently and joyfully look forward to sharing God's glory." We should feel immense pleasure as we hope to partner with God as He works out His glorious plan in and through our lives now and forever.

It was the venerable scholar W. E. Vine who defined the word *hope* in the New Testament as "the happy anticipation of good." Hope is the happy feeling we get when we think about the good things God has planned for our future, in view of His plans for the future of a redeemed world.

Jonathan Edwards is considered by many to be the greatest philosopher and theologian in American history. He was a pastor and revivalist—a leader in the Great Awakening of 1742—and a brilliant intellectual force. When he died, he was the president of Princeton University. In a quest to find a "unifying theory of everything," he wrote an ambitious book called *The End for Which God Created the World*. In this work, Edwards taught us that God is completely happy in himself. Ben Stevens, in his wonderfully accessible adaptation of this classic, *Why God Created the World*, has Edwards writing that "God is glorious and happy, independent of any external circumstances." He is everything true and good and beautiful, and He had everything He needed before He created the world. But He wanted to share His glory. He wanted a bigger audience to witness who He is and what He does. He was so happy that He didn't want to keep His happiness to himself. Thus, He created the world to expand himself and multiply himself and to create a bigger audience for himself. God is so glorious—so unmitigatedly happy—that He made the entire universe so there would be created beings He could invite into His happiness.

There was a deep connection in Edwards' mind between an individual's happiness and the glory of God. God intended that when we see Him—when we witness who He is and what

He does—we participate in His happiness. "A sight of God, Edwards tells us, is 'happifying' . . . it causes happiness to well up on the inside of a person. . . . Seeing God fulfills the design of humanity and therefore sets the heart and mind into motion—it happifies." This is almost too much for me to comprehend, but I grasp enough of it to know that through a relationship with God I can experience genuine pleasure in light of ultimate meaning. I literally share in His happiness.

To be happy, then, I should focus my attention on God. As Edwards poignantly said, a sight of God "happifies." Though we cannot see God now as we will see Him in the age to come, we can—through His Spirit—look at Him now. "And we all, who with unveiled faces contemplate the Lord's glory, are being transformed into his image with ever-increasing glory, which comes from the Lord, who is the Spirit." If we will contemplate Him, we will become more and more like Him and experience His ever-increasing glory in our lives.

I have recited a lot of contemporary science of happiness research in this chapter that shows us the benefits that accrue to happy people. But here is the ancient wisdom that undergirds all of that. God created people to share His happiness, and if we will focus our attention on Him, we will experience His happiness more and more. This seemingly ethereal truth is the most practical thing I know to say to promote happiness in our lives.

If, as a leader, I am obligated to be happy, then I am obligated—privileged!—to look at God. How do we look at God? We look at Him when we practice spiritual disciplines such as contemplative prayer, Scripture reading, and meditation.

I particularly like to talk about meditation in this context: Christ-centered meditation is focused thought on God, His world, His Word, and His Word to us. In Christian meditation we do not lose our personhood—as some meditative practices suggest—but rather focus on the person of God and therefore become more like Him as persons in relationship with Him.

We do not meditate in order to escape this world, but rather to partner with God to engage in this world and change it for the better. We do not meditate to empty our minds but rather to fill our minds with the thoughts of God. Through meditation we contemplate God and are changed to be more like Him.

Research is revealing that when we meditate, we transform our minds. Dr. Kelly McGonigal, a health psychologist who teaches at Stanford University, tells us that "neuroscientists have discovered that when you ask the brain to meditate, it gets better not just at meditating, but at a wide range of self-control skills, including attention, focus, stress management, impulse control, and self-awareness. . . ." Shawn Achor writes that "research even shows that regular meditation can permanently rewire the brain to raise levels of happiness, lower stress, even improve immune function." David Brooks informs us that when we think a thought often enough, it's like a wire automatically appears between two cell phones that frequently call one another. We wire our brains with our thoughts. We become what we repeatedly think. And evidently meditation is so powerful that it literally changes the very structure of our brains if we meditate just ten to fifteen minutes a day.

> Hospitable leadership is a state of being that welcomes people to who we are and what we are doing.

Imagine the power of regular and focused thought on God. A Being who is in such a state of happiness that creation provided Him with an opportunity to overflow His pleasure—to fill the whole world with His glory. It's as if He says to us, "Look at me. I will rewire your brain and transform your very being into an ever-increasing state of joy." As the psalmist taught us, "Blessed is the one . . . whose delight is in the law of the Lord, and who meditates on his law day and night . . . whatever they do prospers."

I asserted earlier that emotions are contagious. That we impart emotions to one another. That being true, I want to make certain that I am in a position to catch the emotional contagion of a happy God. I want to share in my Master's happiness. I must also be happy so I can invite those I am leading to share in my happiness as well. Hospitable leadership is a state of being that welcomes people to who we are and what we are doing. This is what God does, and I believe that this is what He expects of those of us who lead.

I accept the responsibility to be happy. And I accept the responsibility to create environments in which those I lead are inspired to happiness as well. The time to be happy is now.

Leadership Take-Homes

1. **Happiness creates the conditions for success.** Hospitable leaders should strive to be happy and to create an environment conducive to the happiness of those we lead. Happy is God's state of being, and He invites us to join Him in it.

2. **Find happiness in the scope of eternity.** Connecting our action with our God-inspired destiny facilitates peak joy.

3. **Seeing God "happifies."** We can look at God through prayer, Scripture reading, and meditation. Emotions are contagious; as leaders, we want to catch God's happiness and pass it on.

Sources

"There is no duty": Leo Buscaglia, *Loving Each Other* (Thorofare: SLACK, 1984), 110.

"Come and share your master's happiness!": Matthew 25:21.

"We should . . . think that": Dallas Willard, *The Divine Conspiracy: Rediscovering Our Hidden Life in God* (New York: Harper Collins, 1997), 62–63.

"blessed God": 1 Timothy 1:11 ASV.

"blissful God": 1 Timothy 1:11 ABUV from *The Bible from 26 Translations* (Moss Point, MS: Mathis Publishers, 1993), 2420.

"happy God": 1 Timothy 1:11 EB.

"Happiness leads to success": Shawn Achor, *The Happiness Advantage: The Seven Principles of Positive Psychology That Fuel Success and Performance at Work* (New York: Crown Publishing, 2010), 21.

Happy people in business produce higher profits: Shawn Achor, "Positive Intelligence," *Harvard Business Review*, January-February 2012.

"how happy individuals were": C. S. Dweck, *Mindset: The New Psychology of Success* (New York: Ballantine, 2006), 7.

Emotions—both positive and negative—are contagious.: Shawn Achor, *The Happiness Advantage*, 205.

"Like secondhand smoke, the leakage of emotions": Daniel Goleman, *Social Intelligence: The New Science of Human Relationships* (New York: Bantam, 2006), 14.

"The power to spark emotional contagion": Shawn Achor, *The Happiness Advantage*, 208.

"sadness as an emotion" . . . "enough 'true' smiles": Kevin Randall, "Teams Turn to a Face Reader, Looking for that Winning Smile," *The New York Times*, December 25, 2014, https://www.nytimes.com/2014/12/26/sports/nba-bucks-looking-for-an-edge-hire-expert-in-face-time.html.

"Riches and honors": Arthur Brooks, "Love People, Not Pleasure, and Happiness Will Follow," *New York Times*, July 20, 2014, 1:6.

"the overall experience of pleasure and meaning": Dr. Tal Ben-Shahar, *Happier* (New York: McGraw, 2007), 33.

"pleasure combined with deeper feelings": Shawn Achor, *The Happiness Advantage*, 39.

"Since we have been made right with God": Romans 5:1–2 NCV.

"absolute wholeness—full, harmonious": Tim Keller, *The Reason for God* (New York: Dutton, 2008), 464.

"This happened through our Lord Jesus Christ": Romans 5:1–2 NCV.

"and we are happy because of the hope": Romans 5:2 NCV.

"we are the most miserable people in the world": 1 Corinthians 15:19 NLT (1996).

"happy": Romans 5:2 NCV.

"rejoice": Romans 5:2 KJV.

"exult": Romans 5:2 NASB.

"confidently and joyfully look forward to sharing": Romans 5:2 NLT.

"the happy anticipation of good.": W. E. Vine, *Vine's Expository Dictionary of Biblical Words* (Nashville: Thomas Nelson, 1985), 311.

"unifying theory of everything": Ben Stevens, *Why God Created the World* (Colorado Springs: NavPress, 2014), 127.

"God is glorious and happy": Stevens, 11.

"There was a deep connection in Edwards'": John Piper, *Don't Waste Your Life* (Wheaton: Crossway Books, 2003), 29.

"A sight of God, Edwards tells us": Kyle Strobel, *Formed for the Glory of God* (Downers Grove: InterVarsity Press, 2013), 23.

"And we all, who with unveiled faces": 2 Corinthians 3:18.

"neuroscientists have discovered that": Kelly McGonigal, *The Willpower Instinct* (New York: Avery-Penguin, 2013), 24–25.

"research even shows that regular": Shawn Achor, *The Happiness Advantage*, 52.

Evidently meditation is so powerful: Shawn Achor, "Positive Intelligence," 100.

When we think a thought often enough: David Brooks, *The Social Animal* (New York: Random House, 2011), 47, 49–51.

"Blessed is the one": Psalm 1:1–3.

14

Always Hope for More

I t is difficult to overstress how essential it is for a hospitable leader to practice a disciplined hope. Our entire being responds to hope, transforming the overall atmosphere of our life and leadership in incalculably favorable ways. An overwhelming amount of scientific research details that our very physiology reacts positively to hope. When we hope, for instance, the neurotransmitter dopamine is released, which helps us increase focus on what we hope for, and moves us to take action toward our dreams. As we hope, serotonin and endorphins pump through our system and we feel pleasure and sometimes even euphoria. Thinking hopeful thoughts literally changes the structure of our brain—and shapes our very DNA—in a propitious direction. Hope is a dopamine-producing, serotonin-releasing, endorphin-level-raising, brain-restructuring, DNA-shaping, happiness-elevating miracle drug.

We ought not be surprised at the power of hope. The wisest man who ever lived wrote that "the hopes of the godly result in happiness." In the previous chapter I encouraged us to focus our thoughts on God, His world, His Word, and His Word to us in order to share in His happiness. When we fix our eyes on Him—who He is and what He does—it produces hope. And regardless of our present circumstance, hope results in happiness.

We do not become happy because we make life about ourselves and get up every day chasing happiness. Dr. Suzanne Segerstrom, who won the Templeton Positive Psychology Prize for her work on the science of optimism, advocates passionately for the proven benefits of happiness. Yet she insists the research shows that people who get up every day with happiness as their primary goal will probably not be very happy. Happiness is found when we are full of hope and when hope moves us to fully engage in a life of purpose. When we hope, we feel pleasure in the framework of a meaningful life. Again, as Paul wrote to the Romans, "We are happy because of the hope we have of sharing in God's glory."

> **Happiness is found when we are full of hope and when hope moves us to fully engage in a life of purpose.**

If we want to be happy, we must pay careful attention to our hope levels. Doris Kearns Goodwin eloquently recounts how President Abraham Lincoln traveled from Washington, D.C., to visit General Ulysses Grant and the Union troops as they confronted the Confederate army at Petersburg, Virginia. It was the summer of 1864, several years into the bloody war that had ravaged the Unites States. Lincoln had suffered immensely as he had labored to save the Union and had been ill-served by a succession of generals who seemed unable to deliver final victory. He was excited to visit Grant and his troops and believed that the long-elusive victory was imminent. He was welcomed by exultant soldiers including a brigade of black soldiers, newly emancipated, "who rushed forward to greet the president, 'screaming, yelling, shouting: Hurrah for the Liberator; Hurrah for the President.' Their 'spontaneous outburst' moved Lincoln to tears, 'and his voice was so broken by emotion' that he could hardly reply." He spent time with Grant, who told him just what he wanted to hear; "I am just as sure of going into Richmond as I am of any future event. It may take a long summer day, but I will go in." All in all, the president "found the army in fine health good position and good spirits." The president returned to Washington, strengthened in his confidence in General Grant, the army, and the future of the Union.

Goodwin then insightfully comments on the importance of this visit. "Acutely aware of his own emotional needs, Lincoln had chosen exactly the right time to review the troops, for his conversations with Grant and his interaction with the soldiers sustained and inspired him during the troubling days ahead." She then quotes Daniel Goleman, who in his landmark work *Emotional Intelligence* wrote that having hope "'means that one will not give in to overwhelming anxiety, a defeatist attitude, or depression in the face of difficult challenges or setbacks.' Hope is 'more than the sunny view that everything will turn out all right'; it is 'believing you have the will and the way to accomplish your goals.' . . . Lincoln understood that numerous setbacks were inevitable before the war could be brought to a close. Yet in the end, he firmly believed the North would prevail."

There was so much at stake that as a leader, President Lincoln was required to stimulate hope, and he instinctively knew this. Though at times during this long war he had felt something approaching despair, he knew he had to take action to raise hope levels—first his own hope, and then the hope of those he was leading. And when he hoped, I believe that he felt pleasure as he thought about the future even during extremely difficult times. That he happily anticipated the good.

I would also say that he was happy when he hoped in light of the glory of God. He was fighting the good fight—doing God's work—accomplishing God's purposes. I'm reminded that it was in this war that Union soldiers were singing the recently composed "Battle Hymn of the Republic": "Mine eyes have seen the glory of the coming of the Lord. . . . Glory, glory, hallelujah! His truth is marching on." Abraham Lincoln hoped that God's glory would be revealed through the success of his efforts to emancipate slaves, save the Union, and fulfill his destiny.

There is a lot at stake in your life if you are a leader, especially if your life is being lived and your leadership is being offered to reveal God's glory. You cannot afford not to be hopeful. You cannot afford not to be happy. You must take the actions necessary to cultivate hope and feel pleasure when you think about your future. And you can. I assure you that if you are unhappy, you can get happy. And if you are happy, you can get happier. We must learn to elevate our hope in God and good.

There are four things I want to emphasize in order to bring this Welcome home: 1) Be at peace with the fact that happiness is experienced in anticipation. 2) Anticipation opens us to possibility. 3) Hope moves us to faith—and when we have faith, possibility becomes reality. 4) Always hope for more. A leader who learns how to raise his or her hope levels lives in a space so heartwarming that people line up to get involved in whatever good thing he or she is hoping to do.

Happiness is in the anticipation. Hope brings us pleasure as we think about our future, regardless of present circumstance. Most of us have read stories about people who won an excess of money in the lottery but are now less happy than they were before they won. Why? Because happiness is not found—at least in the long term—when we get the thing we hope for. "We are happy because of the hope we have. . . ." Dr. Kelly McGonigal informs us that when the brain anticipates something good, it releases dopamine and "we feel alert, awake, and captivated. We recognize the possibility of feeling good and are willing to work for that feeling." Shawn Achor wrote about a study that found "people who just *thought about* watching their favorite movie actually raised their endorphin levels by twenty-seven percent. Often, the most enjoyable part of an activity is in the anticipation."

When we anticipate something, it is as if we are experiencing it. This is so important to remember when we are in the midst of fighting for our God-inspired dreams. The apostle Paul recognized the suffering we all must endure, and encouraged us to taste future glory as we anticipate the better world—and the future feast—that Jesus has promised us. "What we suffer now is nothing compared to the glory he will reveal to us later. . . . All creation anticipates the day when it will join God's children in glorious freedom from death and decay. . . . And even we Christians, although we have the Holy Spirit within us as a foretaste of future glory, also groan to be released from pain and suffering . . . we eagerly look forward to this freedom. For if you already have something, you don't need to hope for it. But if we look forward to something we don't have yet, we must wait patiently and confidently. . . . And we know that God causes everything to work together for the good of those who love God and are called according to his purpose for them." I must not wait to be happy until what I hope for happens. Happiness is in the anticipation—even in the waiting, the groaning, the eagerly looking forward—and in the knowing that God is working everything together for good in my life now and forever.

> A leader who learns how to raise his or her hope levels lives in a space so heartwarming that people line up to get involved in whatever good thing he or she is hoping to do.

When I write about hope in God and His purposes, and the happiness that hope brings, I am not promoting some Pollyanna naïveté. Paulette Zirpoli is an amazing woman in my congregation who has been stricken with amyotrophic lateral sclerosis (ALS). I can't even begin to imagine what she is suffering. She is confined to a wheelchair and can only "speak" by using her eyes to type out letters and words on a screen positioned directly in front of her.

I visited her and her husband, Steve, recently, and she smiled a beautiful smile at me and typed the words "I am so happy" on the screen. How can she be happy? She would gladly tell you, in the most literal terms, that she is happy because of the hope she has of sharing in God's glory. She knows that God could miraculously intervene in her life at any moment, and she hopes for that. She also anticipates the day when her body will be gloriously set free from death and decay. When she thinks about that, she tastes future glory. That's why she can suffer and still say, "I am so happy."

We can extrapolate from this big-picture, future-glory anticipation anything we hope for in line with God's glory now. Anything God has put in our heart but that we have not yet experienced. We must picture that good thing in our mind now and feel pleasure. Foretaste it. Preconceive it. Predict it. Foretell it. Prophesy it. Feast on it!

I think that the discipline of hope is essential to disciplined leadership. We must constantly convey hope to those we are leading, particularly during those times when we have to *make* ourselves hope. Those times when it seems what we hope for is never going to happen. Or perhaps did not happen, at least in exactly the way we had hoped. We must be willing to realistically assess discouraging circumstances while sitting on the edge of our seats in anticipation of a better future.

I challenge us to lead from a place of anticipation in spite of the disappointments and setbacks and struggles and pain inherent to the present human experience and inevitable when leading a worthy cause. People want to partner with a leader who is full of hope for good and for what's next.

Anticipation opens us to possibility. When we are happy, we literally, physically see more of what is around us. More important, when we are in a hopeful emotional state, the eyes of our heart see more clearly.

Positive emotions bathe our brains with "chemicals that not only make us feel good, but dial up the learning centers of our brains to higher levels," wrote Achor. Consequently, we "think more quickly and creatively, become more skilled at complex analysis and problem solving, and see and invent new ways of doing things." This brings to mind the powerful prayer in Ephesians: "I pray that the eyes of your heart may be enlightened in order that you may know the hope to which he has called you," or "I pray that your hearts will be flooded with light so that you can understand the confident hope he has given to those he called." A warm heart sees better. Hope shines light on possibility.

"Possibility is a hint from God," asserted Søren Kierkegaard. Hospitable leaders must be hospitable to possibility. Only when we see what is possible—and help those we lead see what is possible—can we make choices and take actions to lead ourselves and others to preferred futures. Hopeful leaders—happy leaders—are simply more attuned to possibility.

Hope moves us to faith. I have stood near the finish line of the New York City Marathon on several occasions. Not as a runner, but as a fan. My wife loves to run and has completed this iconic marathon several times, as well as several others. I don't think I have ever seen anyone slow down once they see the finish line. In fact, almost everyone speeds up.

At about 26.1 miles into a 26.2-mile marathon, a flood of endorphins and other chemicals are released in their brain, which powers an acceleration to finish the race. This place is called the X-spot. Amazingly, it's also the most likely place for a heart attack to occur. Of course endorphins are flowing before the race and during the race, but this super-rush of endorphins near the end of the race is almost more than a body can take. When we see "success is not only possible but now probable, the reaction is physically powerful. . . . Of course, this phenomenon doesn't occur only in sports. No matter what your goal is—whether it's finishing a marathon, completing a big project at work, or losing twenty pounds—your brain behaves in the exact same way. As soon as your brain registers that you are going to achieve your goal, it releases these same chemicals that give you the extra boost you need to accelerate." I like to think that when possibility becomes probability, I have a positive "heart attack" of sorts: my heart begins pounding with faith-filled expectation.

There is something infinitely powerful that happens to us spiritually—and therefore throughout our entire being—when what we hope for turns into something we are certain of. "Now faith is being sure of what we hope for, being convinced of what we do not see." Hope, potent as it is, becomes something even more effective when it turns into faith. When we intentionally hope, at some point there is a kind of spiritual X-spot where we move from hoping for something to being flooded with knowing that what we hope for is a certainty. "Against all hope, Abraham in hope believed and so became the father of many nations."

Hoping for something good is useful to any person. Hope raises our happiness levels and helps us move toward what we hope for. This is a part of natural law. But when hope turns to faith in God and His promises, something supernatural happens. Why? God responds to faith. Hope creates an environment that is hospitable to all kinds of good things. And maybe the best thing is that hope makes room for faith to be activated and, when we exercise faith, God responds by doing things only He can do. Hope moves us to act. Faith moves God to act.

That's when the impossible becomes possible and the possible becomes probable and real.

We must always hope for more. When we create hospitable environments infused with hope and happiness, we will often get the good that we pray and believe and work for. This brings its own set of perplexities. We must learn to continue to hope even as we get what we hope for and face the unique challenges inherent to success.

Some time ago I was speaking and serving and learning in Rwanda with a group of leaders and pastors from the New York City area. We then went on safari in the great Massai Mara National Reserve in Kenya. Several of us, all men, were in an open-sided jeep. Our guide had found a lion lying in the shade, and we parked about twenty feet from it. We were full of excitement, testosterone, bravado—and ourselves. We had been looking for a lion!

My friend Bryan's video camera recorded the scene. The lion lies there yawning. We are laughing and talking like giddy high-school sophomores. One voice says, "Here, kitty kitty." Laughter. Another voice, "Here, kitty kitty kitty." Before long, a chorus of voices call the big cat. And then it stands and stares toward us, and starts moving directly at us. The camera begins to shake. The jeep rocks violently as we shift in the opposite direction from the stalking lion. The huge animal brushes by the front of the jeep but the camera does not capture this. The camera is whirling around wildly, pointing at everything but the lion. Then we see its hindquarters as it gracefully walks into a grove of trees beyond us. The sound is the nervous laughter of men reminded that some things require a healthy respect—and a serious dose of caution.

This has become a stark mental picture for me. What happens when we get what we ask for—when we want something and it comes to us and we are frightened by it? Like when the apostle Paul wrote that "a great door for effective work has opened to me, and there are many who oppose me." We got what we hoped for . . . now what? Getting what we hope for often has unintended consequences.

A young woman hopes to be married. She prays, "God, please give me a husband." It is a worthy prayer. God gives her a husband. A year later, the same woman prays, "God, why did you give me this husband?" Alan Loy McGinnis wrote, "I do not know any way one can stay happily married . . . without some willingness to suffer." New levels of suffering often accompany answered prayer.

A young couple desires children and eventually has them. As the years move forward, they discover, as all parents do, that the children they hoped for have become their greatest source of earthly joy—and tribulation and pain.

An entrepreneur strives optimistically to develop a new business model and does. There is an initial and profound rush of victory. The victory is followed by years of perplexities: how to raise the capital to fund this new opportunity, how to staff it, how to operate it, how to bring sustainability to it, how to scale it, and how to replicate it. Years of challenges are often interwoven with years of new victories.

Christian mystic Teresa of Avila said, "There are more tears shed over answered prayers than unanswered ones." Oscar Wilde expressed similar sentiments when he wrote that "in this world there are only two tragedies. One is not getting what one wants, the other is getting it."

I have mentioned several times in this Welcome that Paul told the Romans that "we are happy because of the hope we have of sharing God's glory." We should also note that he goes on to say, "Not only so, but we also glory in our sufferings, because we know that suffering produces perseverance; perseverance, character; and character, hope. And hope does not put us to shame."

It is interesting that happiness and hope are mentioned in the same breath as suffering, perseverance, character, and then again hope. Suffering, and the need to persevere, and the character that deepens if we do, is part of life for all of us. I also consider this: Sometimes when we hope, we get what we hope for and have to suffer—persevere—and build character to get to more hope. I'm talking specifically now about the kind of suffering that comes when we try to do good. "But even if you should suffer for what is right, you are blessed. . . . For it is better, if it is God's will, to suffer for doing good than for doing evil."

Regardless of our circumstance, we can't ever lose hope. In fact, we must always hope for more. We will be happy as we hope and happy after we get the thing we hope for and happy as we hope for more. The secret is to practice a disciplined hope in every condition.

I practice the discipline of hope as an intentional part of contemplative prayer and meditation. I focus on God and what we are doing together, and I also force my mind to imagine good things that I hope will come to pass. And when I do, pleasure floods my being. It's as if I swallowed a happiness pill. My entire person responds to hope.

This has been especially helpful during seasons of challenge. Forgive me, but one more reference to the ten-year-long building and property development project I have mentioned a couple of times already—years of negotiations, zoning boards, planning boards, Town Council meetings, not-in-my-backyard neighbors, architects, engineers, contractors, building inspectors, bureaucrats, raising money, borrowing money, needing more money . . . There were many days when the obstacles were so great that it looked like this part of our dream would never happen.

But during times of prayer and meditation—sometimes lying in bed in a dark room in the middle of the night—I would make myself practice hope as a deliberate discipline. I would imagine sitting at a stoplight, waiting to turn up a road, neither of which yet existed except in my mind. I would imagine the sound of my turn signal blinking, and the light changing from red to green. I would imagine turning left up the road and passing a pond—a waterfall—and a beautiful building that looked like our architects' renderings. I would imagine pulling into a parking space—"my" parking space. I would imagine turning off the car—the engine stopping, opening the door, the creak of the springs, the door slamming shut, and the sound of my own shoes on the concrete walk. I would imagine walking through a doorway into a warm, welcoming building that existed only in my mind—and God's mind. And Jesus would meet me there.

As I would discipline myself to think those thoughts, discouragement would turn to joy. I shared in my Master's happiness. Dopamine, endorphins—whatever all the science says—flooded my being. I felt pleasure. Happiness. And why not? I am happy when I hope for good things in my future in line with God's glory.

I sense that people everywhere are longing for hope and the happiness hope brings. Someone has to lead people to what they long for. What could happen if a multitude of leaders in every sphere of our society would see the cultivation and conveyance of hope as a critical leadership practice? What if those of us who are leading got up every day and insisted that regardless of the provocations we face, we have a moral obligation to be happy—to welcome others into our blessed state—and to lead from that pleasant place. This is central to what hospitable leaders do.

> **Our world needs leaders who, like Jesus, sit in the middle of a great celebration and invite people in.**

When we hope from the future back, we stimulate happiness now that is based in what is eternally important and real. If we are happy, our leadership domain can in fact feel like a feast that a father prepared for his son.

My prayer for you, dear reader, is that "God, who gives you hope, will keep you happy and full of peace as you believe in him. May you overflow with hope through the power of the Holy Spirit."

Our world needs leaders who, like Jesus, sit in the middle of a great celebration and invite people in. Who help people feel home. Who make everyone—especially strangers—feel welcome. Who are hospitable to dreamers and their dreams. Who speak the truth seasoned with grace. And who are full of hope and happiness and enjoy the feast of life. Hospitable leaders. Our world needs leaders like you.

Leadership Take-Homes

1. **Practice a disciplined hope.** We must relentlessly cultivate our hope in God and good. "The hopes of the godly result in happiness."

2. **A hopeful environment makes room for faith to be activated.** When we exercise faith, God responds by doing things only He can do.

3. **Our world needs hopeful, happy, welcoming leaders who offer a feast for those they lead.** Like Jesus' leadership, ours also can feel like a feast we have prepared for those we lead.

Sources

Hope is a dopamine: Dr. Caroline Leaf, *Switch On Your Brain* (Grand Rapids: Baker Books, 2013), 19, 35.

"the hopes of the godly result in happiness.": Proverbs 10:28 NLT.

Research shows that people who get up every day with happiness as their primary goal will probably not be very happy.: Dr. Suzanne Segerstom, *Breaking Murphy's Law: How Optimists Get What They Want from Life—and Pessimists Can Too* (New York: The Guilford Press, 2006), 1–7.

"We are happy because of the hope we have.": Romans 5:2 NCV.

"who rushed forward to greet": Doris Kearns Goodwin, *Team of Rivals: The Political Genius of Abraham Lincoln* (New York: Simon & Schuster, 2005), 629–631.

"Mine eyes have seen the glory": Julia Ward Howe, "Battle Hymn of the Republic," public domain.

"we feel alert, awake, and captivated": Dr. Kelly McGonigal, *The Willpower Instinct: How Self-Control Works, Why It Matters, and What You Can Do to Get More of It* (New York: Avery, Penguin, 2013), 112.

"people who just *thought about*": Shawn Achor, *The Happiness Advantage: The Seven Principles of Positive Psychology That Fuel Success and Performance at Work* (New York: Crown Publishing, 2010), 52.

"What we suffer now is nothing compared to": Romans 8:18–28 NLT (1996).

"chemicals that not only make us feel good": Shawn Achor, *The Happiness Advantage*, 44.

"I pray that the eyes of your heart may be enlightened": Ephesians 1:18.

"I pray that your hearts will be flooded with light so that you can understand": Ephesians 1:18 NLT.

"Possibility is a hint from God.": Søren Kierkegaard, *The Journals of Kierkegaard*, www.archive.org/details/journalsofkierke002379mbp.

"success is not only possible, but now probable": Shawn Achor, *Before Happiness: The 5 Hidden Keys to Achieving Success, Spreading Happiness, and Sustaining Positive Change* (New York: Crown Publishing, 2013), 108–109.

"Now faith is being sure of what we hope for": Hebrews 11:1 NET.

"Against all hope, Abraham in hope believed": Romans 4:18.

"a great door for effective work.": 1 Corinthians 16:9.

"I do not know any way one can stay happily married": Alan Loy McGinnis, *The Romance Factor* (New York: Harper & Row, 1982) 185.

"There are more tears shed after answered prayers": St. Teresa of Avila as quoted by Beca Lewis in *Living in Grace: The Shift to Spiritual Perception* (Encinitas, CA: Perception, 2002), 129.

"in this world there are only two tragedies": Oscar Wilde, *Lady Windermere's Fan,* Act III.

"we are happy because of": Romans 5:2 NCV.

"Not only so, but we also glory": Romans 5:3–5.

"But even if you should suffer": 1 Peter 3:14.

"For it is better, if it is God's will": 1 Peter 3:17.

"God, who gives you hope, will keep you happy": Romans 15:13 NLT (1996).

Acknowledgments

To the people of The Life Christian Church: Thank you for being hospitable to me and my God-inspired dreams for these many years. I think I have learned more from all of you than you have ever learned from me. Our past is glorious. I believe our future is more and better than we have even dreamed of.

To the board and elders at TLCC: Thanks for affording me the liberty of writing this book and for supporting Sharon and me in every conceivable manner.

To the staff team at TLCC: We are a great team! I enjoy the work we do together so much. I could never have written this book—nor do many of the things I am privileged to do—without your partnership. Special thanks to my executive assistants Tanya Atterberry and Evelyn Martinez. You enable me and Sharon to do what we are called to do in so many ways. And an extra special thanks to you, Evelyn, for partnering with me on all things book. You did a great job.

Esther Fedorkevich: I am so blessed to have you as my agent. Many years ago you convinced me to write. I am glad we were able to do this project together. You and your entire team at the Fedd Agency are just fantastic.

To the team at Bethany House: Thank you for your effort and excellence to make this a successful project. Special thanks to you, Kim Bangs, for believing in *The Hospitable Leader* and for providing the leadership to make it happen. And to my editor, Sharon Hodge . . . you made this a better book. I am grateful.

To my family: Thank you, Mom and Dad, for creating a climate in our home that was hospitable to me in every imaginable way. Thank you, Sharon, for your devotion to our family. You are the personification of hospitality. Sumerr, Caleb, and Christian, I am so proud of you. Being your mom's husband and your dad is the most meaningful part of my life. Also Caleb and Christian, a big thanks to you for reading and re-reading this manuscript and offering your insightful feedback and contributions. And to Amanda, welcome to our family. We are so excited for you and Christian and your future together.

To Jesus Christ: Thank you for more and better life than I could ever dream of.

Terry A. Smith has served as lead pastor of The Life Christian Church for twenty-seven years. TLCC, a nondenominational faith community with campuses in West Orange and Paramus, New Jersey, is known for its vibrant diversity and robust leadership culture, with people from more than 132 distinct communities in the New York City metro area participating in the life of the church.

Terry is a cofounder of The New York City Leadership Center. A gifted communicator, Terry speaks in a variety of venues nationally and internationally and is the author of *Live Ten: Jump Start the Best Version of Your Life*. He holds a bachelor of science in organizational management (church studies) and a master of arts in organizational leadership.

Terry has been married to his wife, Sharon, for thirty-five years, and they have three adult children: Sumerr, Caleb, and Christian.

www.TerryASmith.com

 @terry_a_smith
 @PastorTerryASmith
@terry_a_smith